Tales of
HOLLYWOOD
the
BIZARRE

Tales of
HOLLYWOOD
the
BIZARRE

Unexplained Deaths • Oscar Rip Offs
Blacklisting • Tragedies • Erotomania
Sexual Harassment • Devil Worship
And Other Vicious Exploitation

by

John Austin

A division of Shapolsky Publishers, Inc.

S.P.I. BOOKS

A division of Shapolsky Publishers, Inc.

For any additional information, contact:

S.P.I. BOOKS/Shapolsky Publishers, Inc.
136 West 22nd Street
New York, NY 10011
212/633-2022 / FAX 212/633-2123

10 9 8 7 6 5 4 3 2 1

ISBN: 1-56131-142-X

Design and typography by Smith, Inc., NYC
Manufactured in the United States of America

For L.S.F. . . .

The first stabilizing
entity in my life. . .
May it always be so. . .

*"You are the angel glow that lights
a star / The dearest things I know are
what you are."* *

*Jerome Kern/Oscar Hammerstein
All The Things You Are

OTHER BOOKS BY
JOHN AUSTIN

More Of . . . Hollywood's Unsolved Mysteries

Hollywood's Unsolved Mysteries

The World I Live In: The George Jessel Story

Sex Is Big Business

How To Syndicate To Newspapers & Magazines

Surrogate (with Holly Hill)

ACKNOWLEDGMENTS

. . .are due to those who
manage to make books like this possible.
We believe we have managed to spell the names
correctly. To many,
that is all that really matters.

As one Hollywood wit remarked,
"Pan me, boys, but please don't ignore me!"
We have tried not to.
If we have, it was inadvertent and we'll try to remedy
the oversight in the next volume.

bi-zarre (bi zar`) adj. Markedly
unusual in appearance, style, OR
GENERAL CHARACTER; whimsically
strange; odd: BIZARRE [clothing]
BEHAVIOR.

— *Random House Dictionary*

Contents

Tales of
HOLLYWOOD
the
BIZARRE

CHAPTER ONE

Behind the Tinsel, Glitter and Glamor

"We did as we damn well pleased . . ."
— **Clara Bow**
The "It Girl"

Hollywood has, over the years, screened many fantastic and original—and not so original— stories. From the silent era through the special effects of the 1990s, its magic has entertained masses throughout the world. Perhaps no other "pay per view" medium —with the possible exception of television—has entertained so many for so little cost. Stars have loomed bigger than life on 20-foot screens in darkened theatres and drive-ins, in 747s plying the skies of the world, on ships at sea, and wherever enough power exists to light a projector.

But, behind the tinsel, glitter and glamor of what appears on the silver screen, dozens of tragic stories exist—never seen by the film-going public. Heartache, divorce, assorted mayhem committed against stars and members of the film community—even murder by the crazed "fans" who claim to adore them for their glamorous, beautiful existences.

Working in Hollywood — from stars to technicians — is a rough occupation. For those in front of the camera, it is a heart-breaking life which taxes the moral fiber of the most stout-hearted and ambitious. Many times, bizarre suicide and death in strange ways have claimed those who never caught the brass ring, or caught it for only a fleeting moment.

In the beginning, Cecil B. DeMille disembarked from a train in Phoenix in 1913 and found it raining there. He caught the next train for "the coast" to shoot *The Squaw Man*. Ever since, "the coast" has been a center for misfits, fortune seekers, con-men, hangers-on, sycophants and people of dubious gender, as well as those who successfully caught the public's attention and fancy with their images on "the silver screen" and their names in the "fan" magazines.

Hollywood thrived on power, money and the press. For over seventy years, the "control" of the entertainment press of Hollywood has been fed by big money, backed by studio power. In the beginning, total control was maintained by threat of banishment for non-compliance. Even today, accessibility means compliance and Hollywood is seldom written about subjectively.

In 1922, the country was rocked when comedian/star Fatty Arbuckle was accused of the rape and murder of Virginia Rappe. Arbuckle had recently signed a $3 million contract, roughly the equivalent of the $30 million a Sly Stallone or Bruce Willis could command in today's market. Though Arbuckle was acquitted following his third trial (the first two ended with no verdicts), the public never learned that Adolph Zukor, the very man who had signed the contract, had been in collusion with politicians running for re-election and the District Attorney of San Francisco to frame his own star.

Zukor got his way. The public could no longer accept Arbuckle as the rotund comedian they had adored. Theatres would no longer exhibit his two and three reel comedies. Zukor managed to cancel his contract, utilizing an obscure clause in the document.

Zukor was a perfect example of Hollywood in the twenties: a cesspool of vice, a self-contained, oligarchical community which did what it wanted, ignoring public opinion, bribing police and public officials to sweep scandals, felonies, misbehavior and murder under the hand-woven, expensive rugs of the costly Spanish style homes of the film colony. Built with new found wealth, fostered by a nickel-on-the-dollar income tax, the huge mansions sprouted over the foothills of Beverly Hills, Brentwood and Pacific Palisades.

Following the Arbuckle scandal, Will H. Hays, a former Postmaster-General and hack politician, was appointed the "Morals Czar" of Hollywood. Eager to please studio money and power, he established "The Hays Office." Today, an offshoot of "The Hays Office"—the Motion Picture Association of America—still controls access to a journalist's accreditation to "cover" the industry.

Hays, under the pretense of controlling the morals of the industry, was generally more successful in managing to hush up its behind-the-scenes scandals. In several instances, he failed—notably in both the non-suicide of Paul Bern, Jean Harlow's impotent husband, and Harlow's own death five years later from a beating she had received from Bern on their wedding night.

Hollywood—The Bizarre will look at the many antics of the stars—actors and actresses—and the industry in general which, taken as a whole, reveal a perverse, self-centered and closed society which flaunts morality, social customs and laws with the belief that it can do anything and get away with it. In many cases, it has, it can and it does.

Early producers in the silent era—and even into the sound era—poured acid in each other's developers and hired gunman—mostly out of work cowboys—to put bullets through camera lenses. Mack Sennett turned two zany comedians loose in a Shriners' parade, completely disrupting it, thereby supplying a comedy scene with a thousand unpaid extras. One hoydenish star publicly dipped her breasts in champagne and invited her gentlemen friends—as well as a few strangers—to lick off the wine. Elinor Glyn—the queen of sex novelists—insisted that King of the Cowboys Rex Bell had more "It" than his wife Clara Bow. Mabel Normand delayed her wedding to Lew Cody while she questioned the minister on how he kissed wedded brides. And the inimitable Cecil B. DeMille insisted that actor H.B. Warner—playing Christ in the original *King of Kings*

—be treated with the reverence due to the real deity. De Mille, however, thought nothing of scorching Warner's hide with the most blasphemous of language when the actor muffed a scene.

Actors stole, swapped and abandoned wives, husbands and mistresses by the score. They murdered each other and died raving dope fiends. Some became nuns—and monks. They were alternately devout and profane. . .crazy and sane.

Hollywood in its heyday—in the days when studio moguls, the brothers Warner, San Goldwyn, Zukor, Harry Cohn, Louis B. Mayer, Darryl Zanuck and Joe Schenck ruled—was a city of clowns. But, as all funnymen are fond of stressing, comedy is but slightly removed from tragedy.

Tears frequently flowed; the star who was the happiest in public was often the one who cried the bitterest in private.

"We did as we damn well pleased," Clara Bow told an interviewer.

The phrase summed up Hollywood's attitude.

And they did as they damn well pleased. They divorced their real lives and tried to continue their reel ones off screen. Their lives were filled with false and exaggerated values which caused regret—and ultimate ruin. They still do. From nobodies, they were turned into idols. Men envied them. Women begged to love them and to make love to them. They were smothered in adulation, in money and the things which money could buy—including people. They were all Harun-al-Raschids in a Hollywood Bagdad—with a thousand genies to grant their every wish.

The chaotic result was an endless supply of stories of triumph, defeat, love, hate, scandal, sacrifice and bravery. The greatest—the most magnificent, colossal and stupendous (to use Hollywood's own adjectives)— were those in which great stars were handed roles written by life and directed by Fate.

For people who lived their lives in artificiality, the stars played their real-life roles splendidly and with style. When Arbuckle was handed his tragic role— although it was Hollywood that engineered and destroyed him—he carried it off magnificently and with dignity. And no star ever handled tragedy and heartbreak as touchingly as Mabel Normand handled her role in the murder of William Desmond Taylor (who was later revealed to have homosexual tendencies).

Mary Astor, one of the most beautiful stars of the thirties and forties, faced a damning scandal to fight for what she rightfully believed to be hers.

Astor had written passages in her diary about the "staying power" of George Kaufman, the Broadway playwright with whom she was having a wild affair. When it became known that parts of her diary were to be read in open court as a result of a child custody case, an emergency meeting was convened by Samuel Goldwyn. The group included Harry Cohn, Irving Thalberg, Jack Warner and a Bank of America representative. At the time, Astor was starring in *Dodsworth* for Goldwyn and the Bank of America had a great deal of money invested in Hollywood films. Both the former glove salesman and the banker were becoming very nervous about the box office fate of the film if a full blown scandal about the sex life of its star became fodder for the sob sisters of the Hearst Press and the New York tabloids.

Thalberg strongly advised Astor to give up the fight for her child, not only for her own good, "but for the good of Hollywood as well." The phrase might just as well have read "for the good of *Dodsworth*."

To her credit, Astor adamantly refused to consider the ultimatum. The months she had been separated from her daughter—then in the custody of her husband, Dr. Franklyn Thorpe—had convinced her that regaining the custody of her child was the most important thing in the world to her. "And besides," she said later in her autobiography, "Walter Huston [her co-star in *Dodsworth*] was waiting for me in his dressing room with a bottle of champagne."

Somehow, some passages of the diary were revealed by Hearst's *Herald-Examiner.* One headline read: BARE MARY ASTOR DIARY TELLING KAUFMAN AFFAIR

Fell Like a Ton of Bricks!
Lavender Love Secrets
Book Related!
"In lavender ink, Mary Astor wrote in her diary love secrets of the romantic interludes she experienced with George S. Kaufman.

"Today the attorney for her former husband, Dr. Franklyn Thorpe, released excerpts from the lavender diary. They follow:

"'I am still in a daze—a kind of rosy glow. It is beautiful, glorious and I hope it is my last love. I can't top it with anything in my experience.'"

Immediately afterward, in spite of witnesses for both sides massed in court and ready to testify, Judge Goodwin J. Knight ("Goody" to his friends and to the industry) made a surprising move:

COURT OFFICIALLY HALTS MARY ASTOR'S ROMANTIC STORY headlined the late afternoon editions. Knight had unexpectedly ordered a continuance, stating that he was taking the unusual action to bring the case back into "proper perspective." What he failed to tell participants was that he had been guaranteed the money, hype and push for a later run at the Governorship of California. He was elected—for two terms.

When the court reconvened, Knight ordered that Marilyn Thorpe should spend the nine month school year with her mother and the three month summer vacation with her father.

Knight then ordered the diary impounded in a place known only to himself and his law clerk. It was burned in 1952.

The diary, as we were told many years later by a close associate of "Goody" Knight, contained some very candid opinions and revelations about many

Hollywood people. Only when Knight ordered it impounded did Hollywood, per se, sleep easier. Astor had written the truth about too many of its citizens.

And Hollywood has never been a city where the truth is popular.

Early in the 1930s, as the industry attempted to control news originating within and about itself, editors of newspapers and fan magazines were told that *no stories were to appear without the written permission of the studio publicity department involved.* The Hays Office even insisted that it stamp the back of every "still" photograph used by the studios for publicity purposes. No others were allowed by outside photographers. If any photograph was published without having **Approved for Publication** rubber stamped in purple ink on the back, the magazine or newspaper could be boycotted by the industry, working in unison with the Hays Office. One such imprint from RKO-Radio Pictures—which we still have—reads:

> *"Permission is hereby granted to newspapers, magazines and other periodicals to reproduce this photograph. This is an exclusive photograph, therefore it may not be syndicated, rented or loaned, nor used for any advertising purposes."*

Imprints from other studios were, sometimes, even more stringent, with some even containing the words: *"Written permission must be obtained from [Miracle Pictures] before this photograph can be reproduced."*

Writers with reputations of not adhering to studio "journalism rules" were often barred from studios through the revocation of their Hays Office pasteboards: cards roughly the size of today's credit cards, with a picture identification, the bearer's employer(s) and an admonition to agree to the "Rules of Coverage" laid down by the Hays Office.

These types of censorship illustrate how easily the industry swept causes, reasons and motives under those hand woven rugs. Subtly or heavy-handed, whether overground, underground, via telephone or lunches at the Brown Derby, the industry, spearheaded by the Hays Office, announced that it would brook no interference in its publicized affairs.

William Pine, a publicity director at Paramount Pictures speaking for the industry as a whole, told members of the Press that if their newspapers and magazines "persisted" in printing revealing material regarded by his organization (Paramount) as contrary to its interest, advertising would be cut from their publications and their accreditation "pulled," making it impossible for the "transgressor" to make a living.

It was economic blackmail and total censorship.

It still is. Reporters within the industry today are still considered to be in good standing only when they act as unpaid press agents for the studios—so called employees without portfolios or paychecks. Some of the more unscrupulous reporters have even been known to accept "gratuities" in the form of cash or kind from some studios or their outside press agents for hyping a particular picture or personality.

In this manner, it was — and is — easy for the oligarchy to use its power of economic persuasion to keep its secrets. Universal Pictures managed to keep Rock Hudson's homosexuality under wraps for three decades. When the now defunct magazine *Confidential* dropped a hint to the studio that it was going to publish a story of Rock Hudson cruising the gay bars each evening, the studio instead fed the magazine a story of a similar nature involving a lesser known actor. Thus, it kept Hudson's reputation and box office viability alive, while tossing a fairly unknown actor to the wolves.

Over the years, unusual deaths, accidental homicides, suicides for no apparent reasons and disappearing evidence have been abetted by sycophants who claim to have seen and heard nothing and district attorneys who accepted unusual "honorariums" or campaign contributions for runs at public office. Judge Goodwin J. Knight was only an enthusiastic forerunner.

Through hype, support, expert public relations, free celebrity endorsements and cash, the oligarchy has been marginally responsible for electing three Presidents of the United States.

Hollywood is an oligarchical society in the true sense of the word — a dominant class or clique within a local government structure. It survives on the whims, fads, favors and tastes of the general public, swelling the box office take and increasing ratings on television series. The specialized clique within a clique in television is a special case.

Because of the huge amounts of money generated by the success of those at the "top," Hollywood's best interests are best protected by keeping as much dirty laundry, scandals and behind-the-scenes machinations as possible from the public. Anyone within the industry who tells what he knows, voluntarily or involuntarily, is considered a pariah—an outcast who will afterward find it impossible to obtain work within the industry.

Never was a cover-up more expertly handled than the murder of Marilyn Monroe on the night of August 5, 1962, a cover-up orchestrated and led by the expertise of Hollywood public relations genius Arthur P. Jacobs, and carried out by investigators hired by Hollywood's famed Fred Otash, Peter Lawford and others. After more than thirty years, the truth is finally evolving. But Hollywood, per se, in connection with these powerful and knowledgeable forces, managed to keep Monroe's murder "hush-hush" for almost 25 years.

The public was led to believe that the film goddess committed suicide with an overdose of Nembutal. Nothing was further from the truth. Only a small trace of Nembutal was discovered during the autopsy on her body.

Twenty-five years after the fact, the truth behind Marilyn's death began to emerge, albeit cautiously. Since then, theories have proliferated on practically every tabloid show on television, in the tabloid press and in books.

Perhaps Bob Woodward of *The Washington Post* put it most succinctly about how Hollywood manages to cover up scandals. In his book *Wired,* Woodward wrote that the oligarchy was responsible for events leading up to John Belushi's death from an overdose of cocaine and other designer drugs. He had to defend himself against the attacks of many in the industry, particularly agent Mike Ovitz.

Because Woodward's book about Belushi was honest and objective, Hollywood didn't like it. In his rebuttal to constant attacks by Ovitz, Dan Akroyd and other associates of Belushi, Woodward wrote that if the *Washington Post* covered the nation's capitol like the *Los Angeles Times* covered Hollywood, the *Post* would be out of business in a week.

When employees of the Hollywood studios do talk detrimentally about the industry, they are summarily banished from employment. This was very evident following the *Twilight Zone* trial when director John Landis and several others were tried on manslaughter charges — and acquitted.

The *Twilight Zone* manslaughter case involved the death of actor Vic Morrow and two Vietnamese children. Under California child labor laws, the children were working illegally. There was no "welfare worker" on the set as required by law.

Several members of the crew were subpoenaed to testify by the prosecution and placed under oath on the witness stand. Few have ever again worked in the industry to which they had devoted their lives. One — a top cameraman — told only what he saw — nothing more — under subpoena. He had worked steadily for twenty-six years. He has received only one work call in the last four years.

Fostered by Lea Purwin D'Agostino's weak prosecution, the defendants were acquitted of all charges.

The earnings of major stars and executives are obscene compared to other industries. In itself, this has created an "us against them" mentality in order to protect those earnings. This attitude creates an atmosphere which breeds mystery and isolates its subjects, inviting them — to paraphrase Clara Bow's statement — to do anything they damn well please.

In a broader sense, it also breeds utter contempt for the laws of normal human behavior.

To its own defense, Hollywood — over the years — has been lauded many times and been publicized by many highly paid public relations experts as the center of cinema art. No other film producing country has ever been able to match the expertise and the popularity of films and filmmakers as those with *Made in Hollywood, USA* on the credit crawl.

At the same time, it has been word-painted by writers as Sodom-and-Gomorrah on the Pacific — mainly because those writers did not take the time to learn the ins and outs of a unique industry — an industry with millions of dollars riding on the talents, temperaments and expertise of studio heads, major stars, and world class directors. If any one of them screws up, millions can be lost.

Under such scrutiny, it is not amazing that an oligarchy's good deeds and world wide influence can be forgotten in the heat of a scandal, a murder, a sensational divorce case or the slightest other divertissement.

As you will see in the pages and chapters which follow, Hollywood, per se, is a very strange place which sets its own rules of conduct, of business and of how it punishes those who would transgress against it.

CHAPTER TWO

Albert Dekker...
The Distinguished
was Extinguished

*"There is no streak of
unkindness within him..."*
— **Alfred Lunt**
A lifelong friend

On May 2, 1968, Albert Dekker, still trim
and dapper at 63, and his fiance, Geraldine Saunders,
attended the opening night of Zero Mostel's new play
at Hollywood's Huntington Hartford Theatre. Their
marriage was scheduled for the following month.

Dekker and Saunders made arrangements to go
out again the following evening, but, when "my telephone calls to him on Friday night went unanswered"
and she had not heard from Dekker by Saturday night,
Saunders decided to go to his Hollywood apartment
Sunday morning. Taped or pinned to the front door
were notes from friends who had been unable to contact
Dekker for two days. Saunders pushed a note of her
own under the door. When she returned that evening
and found everything still in place, she went immediately to the manager.

21

Dekker's door had been locked, but not bolted. The apartment seemed in order except for the bathroom door; it was locked from the inside. They forced it open and Saunders fainted.

"It was so horrible," she said later.

The 6'3", 240 pound Dekker was kneeling nude in the bathtub. Dirty, well-used hypodermic needles protruded from each arm. A hangman's noose was around his neck, but not tight enough — according to the coroner's report — to have strangled him. A scarf was tied over his eyes.

Something akin to a horse's bit was in his mouth. Fashioned from a rubber ball and wire, the "bit" had "reins" that were tightly tied behind his head. Two leather thongs were stretched between the leather belts around his neck and chest.

A third belt, around his waist, was tied with a thin rope that stretched to his ankles, where it was secured in some kind of lumber hitch. The end of the rope, which continued up his side, wrapped around his waist several times and was held in Dekker's hands. His wrists were tightly clasped by a set of regulation handcuffs.

Written in lipstick above two needle punctures on his right buttock was the word "whip" and drawings of some sort. Sun rays had been drawn around his nipples. "Make me suck" was written on his thorax; "slave" and "cocksucker" on his chest. Below these was a crude drawing of a woman's vagina. According to the on-scene coroner, the actor had died sometime Friday night. His awkward position had colored his lower body a deep, blood purple. A coroner's aide remarked, "All we need to find now is a vampire's bite!"

During the on-sight investigation, detectives noted no signs of forced entry or struggle. The death was labelled "an indicated suicide. . .quite an unusual one."

Finding no convincing evidence for a suicide, the coroner rejected the detectives' theory. The final report read "accidental death."

Albert Dekker was one of the most cultured actors in the profession. A graduate of Bowdoin College in Maine, he had originally intended to become a psychologist or psychiatrist. However, an alumnus of the college, who happened to be a friend of Alfred Lunt, saw Dekker perform in several college productions and urged him to pursue a career in the theatre. He gave him a letter of introduction to Lunt, at that time one of the most distinguished actors on the American stage.

Dekker made his stage debut in one of Lunt's productions, playing four character roles. By the time he made his film debut ten years later, he was a well-established and popular Broadway star. Lunt, a life long friend, later stated that "Al has a fine mind. There is no streak of unkindness within him."

The blond, blue-eyed actor excelled in character roles and dialects, especially multi-dimensional villains. Dekker often said that he found it more challenging to play a heavy than a hero. He appeared in over 100 films, including *Gentlemen's Agreement, Two Years Before the Mast, East of Eden, Suddenly Last Summer, Beau Geste* and many other classics. His most famous role, and the one for which he is most remembered, was the title role in *Dr. Cyclops,* in which a bald, mad scientist reduced five humans to the size of dolls. *Dr. Cyclops* has become a cult film which is shown regularly on television.

In private life, however, he was a "good" guy, an image of the American family man — and a champion of liberal causes that would later detour his film career for almost twenty years.

In 1929, Dekker married New York actress Esther Guernini. They had two sons and a daughter. He became active in California politics and won a Democratic state assembly seat in 1944. In the assembly, he was known as an ardent supporter of unwed and indigent mothers' rights. He introduced a bill against capital punishment which died in committee. The Hearst press trumpeted it would "take the excitement out of murder trials." Following a discouraging two-year term, he returned to acting.

In the early fifties, Dekker was a triumph on British television with his cultured accent and appearance. He returned to Broadway in the role of Willy Loman in *Death of a Salesman,* a role which was so convincing that his nine-year-old son raced backstage after his suicide scene to make sure his father was still alive. He later won a Tony for his portrayal as the Duke of Norfolk in *A Man For All Seasons* and received rave reviews for his role opposite Spencer Tracy in *Conflict.*

His career plummeted in the mid 1950s when he publicly denounced Senator Joseph McCarthy as a red-baiter and "insane." He began to receive death threats. Though he had served two years in the California State Legislature, his political views were suddenly suspect in Hollywood. He became a possible liability at the box office to any film in which he might appear.

When he was cited by the House Un-American Activities Committee and its counterpart, The California Un-American Activities Committee, he was blacklisted. The committees listed Dekker as a member or "sponsor" of left leaning, Communist "front" organizations such as Youth For Democracy, Citizens Committee for the Motion Picture Strikers, Committee for the First Amendment, Hollywood Democratic Committee, Mobilization for Democracy, Defense of "People's Daily World" and Progressive Citizens of America.

In addition, his wife, Esther, had been a director of the Congress of American Women, at the time considered to be "an out-and-out Communist organization."

Albert Dekker was unable to work in Hollywood or on Broadway for over nineteen years. "All I could do for most of the time," he would later say, "was lecture at colleges and women's clubs."

When his sixteen-year-old son, Jan, died of a self-inflicted, but accidental, gunshot wound, the grief-stricken father tried to explain to friends and the press descending on his Hastings-on-the-Hudson home that "he had been experimenting for over a year on a rifle silencer."

Later, in the rapidly emerging Hollywood liberalism which followed the demise of most of the conservative studio mongols, Dekker would revive his career.

Dekker's shadowy off-screen life surprised everyone — including fiancee Geraldine Saunders, who later went on to achieve fame with *The Love Boat,* which eventually became the long-running television series.

Following the removal of his body, detectives found items of bondage paraphernalia, including leather and rubber clothes, whips, chains and an elaborate library of sado-masochistic pornography. Assorted books and periodicals contained pictures of men and women bound and gagged in bizarre positions. On a desk, in the actor's handwriting, was a long list of bondage details:

Hot wax brushed on nipples and genitals.

Dildoes of all shapes and sizes.

Several 2 inch flat laths or short whips.

Shaving the genitals.

Nipple, ear, nose and penis rings.

Teasing with feathers.

The box with a hole for the head.

The collar suspended from the ceiling.

The buttocks as a pin cushion.

Tied by the neck from a tree.

Legs spread, hands behind, she sitting on the mouth of her slave.

The sexual degrading and abusing of the slave.

Directive to masturbate controlled by the whip.

Forcing the victim to tie himself up.

The admission of surrender and acknowledging the mistress by a signature in blood.

The taboo and the kneeling.

Kissing and sucking the cunt.

Put in frame with buttocks as target painted
in bizarre designs.

Walk through the street tied and naked except
for a raincoat.

Chained by neck and hand.

Subsequent investigations that were never publicized revealed Dekker had vividly and dramatically
dramatized his life experiences. He had participated in
bizarre sexual behavior with friends, including Chinese
acupuncture to the sexual organs, spiritualism, tissue-
extract therapy for potency and sado-masochism.

However, his interest in masochism and bondage
were of recent development. A former girl friend evi-
denced that they had participated in bondage scenes
with the equipment found in the apartment. However,
she had not been with him the night of his death.

Dekker had recently signed to star in a "spaghetti
western" in Italy. He had not appeared visibly depressed
to his friends. His finances were good, although he
had been worried about his health and his failing potency. As mandated under the rules of the Los Angeles
County Coroner's office, a psychiatric "Psychological
Profile" inferred that Dekker died accidentally while
practicing bondage perversion, i.e.: masturbation.

Coroner Noguchi called in a psychologist because
he believed that Albert Dekker had been playing the
most dangerous sex game in the world: a strange ritual
— not uncommon among the Hollywood netherworld
— known as *auto-erotic asphyxia.*

Auto-erotic asphyxia involves hanging oneself for "the ultimate sex thrill." Ritualists *do not* intend to die. Instead, they hope to achieve what they consider the most sublime sexual experience—obtaining orgasm by *risking* death. Inevitably, they handcuff themselves, or bind their hands. Often, they wear blindfolds or hoods. Some don transvestite clothes. The ritual has been described as far back as 1791 by the Marquis de Sade in Justine.

Dr. Joe Rupp, Chief Medical Examiner of Corpus Christi, Texas, and an expert on sex-related deaths, wrote, "Auto-erotic asphyxia is carried on by thousands of individuals who arrive at this practice independently of one another. It represents an as yet unexplored, almost unknown, aspect of human behavior."

Not unexplored to Albert Dekker, who carried it too far. And once too often.

The official coroner's verdict was "Asphyxia due to accidental suffocation."

One question remains unanswered in Albert Dekker's death. According to his fiancee, Dekker had flown home from Mexico after co-starring in Sam Peckinpah's *The Wild Bunch* with his salary of $30,00 *in cash*—demanding to be paid in cash since he claimed to have no bank account at the time.

"We were also about to close a deal in Encino for a house," explained Saunders. "Al was staying alone at the Normandie Street apartment until our house went through escrow. He'd only lived there a week."

According to Saunders, Dekker also had an additional $40,000 in cash from two television roles he had completed before leaving for Mexico. Dekker had felt that a straight cash transaction for the Encino house would be a good bargaining chip, according to his fiancee.

"When he died, there was no trace of the $70,000 anywhere in the apartment," she claimed. Police canvassed banks Dekker had used previously in New York and Los Angeles, but there was no trace of any deposits under his professional spelling of *Dekker,* nor of the legal spelling *Decker.*

Also missing from the apartment was some expensive camera equipment and Dekker's tape recorder, which he was using to prepare himself for a possible role in *Fiddler on the Roof* which he had been offered following the film in Rome.

Toying with the theory that Dekker may have been a closet homosexual who practiced his eccentricities with anonymous male prostitutes, the police made inquiries on the street, but the male hustlers said that Dekker had no reputation among the "street people."

The "male prostitute theory" was thrown out when it was evident that the bathroom door was locked from the inside. Although the chain lock mounted on the inside door jamb was not activated, no one but Dekker could have locked the door.

But why?

Wasn't he alone in the apartment when he decided to practice his auto-eroticism. Did he leave a visitor in the apartment when he locked the bathroom door for privacy? And did the visitor—if there was one—later realize something was wrong, locate the money and equipment and split?

Possible.

If it were not for the locked bathroom door, one could consider that a murderer or accomplice "arranged" the whole bizarre tableau for robbery purposes. But the locked bathroom door precluded any further investigation.

The death of Albert Dekker is closed to further inquiry and the death of the scholarly actor remains a frustrating, confounding mystery—particularly the missing $70,000.

CHAPTER THREE

Sue a Studio—
Never Work
Again

"What we have here is a case about some very weak people blaming someone else for their own inadequacies . . ."
— **Edward Mosk**
Raquel Welch's Attorney

"David Begelman is a killer, and I've got a gun to my head. All I'm saying is he's sending out a letter saying you are in breach of contract and you're in big trouble. He is not going to work around your makeup calls. You are responsible for the delays in the production . . ."

In 1986, on a witness stand in a Los Angeles courtroom, Raquel Welch testified that these words had come from producer Michael Phillips in a telephone call on the night of December 18, 1980.

The next morning, Raquel was scheduled to film her first big dialogue scene in the film *Cannery Row,* a movie she felt would have demonstrated that she could handle challenging, dramatic roles and would mark a transition in her career.

After receiving what she described as Phillips'

"hysterical" telephone call, "I fell into a flood of tears," she said. "I was quite ruined and was sick to my stomach."

Her dramatic testimony concluded the first day of proceedings in Welch's $10 million law suit against Metro-Goldwyn-Mayer, charging breach of contract and defamation of character. She had been fired from the film of John Steinbeck's novel of fishermen in Monterey, California, and immediately replaced by Debra Winger.

The law suit promised to be a rocky ride. For the studio — and for Raquel's career in films.

Welch refused to let the matter rest as more prudent actors would have done if they wished to ever again work in Hollywood. She took the unusual route of publicly challenging David Begelman, a self-admitted forger and president of MGM at the time of her firing; director David Ward; producer Michael Phillips and several John and Jane Does named as defendants. By filing the suit, she hoped to vindicate her professional reputation.

She succeeded, but, in spite of several successful outings on Broadway, Raquel Welch has never made another film.

"My ex-wife, Raquel Welch, knows what she wants and will go to any extremes to get it. She can either be a great lady, a pain in the ass or the bitch of the world."

Her ex-husband, Patrick Curtis, made that statement to us several years before the law suit was filed. As an example, Curtis cited for us the Royal Command Film Performance in London in March, 1966, attended by many international stars of the film and theatre, including the late Rex Harrison, Peter O'Toole and Julie Christie.

"Raquel was just becoming well-known at the time and received a 'command' to appear. She decided, with my help, to wear a modest white dress with just a little cleavage, but it did make her stand out. With all the other big names at that event, it was Raquel who was photographed by, I think, every photographer in London while shaking hands with the Queen of England."

The following day Raquel Welch's picture, in her simple white dress, appeared in every London and provincial newspaper.

"I was accused," said Curtis, "by everyone in the industry — and by the London newspapers in editorials — of manipulating that photograph and arranging to have it printed to the exclusion of all others."

Curtis admitted the picture had been "manipulated," but by Raquel herself. Together, they had discussed the approach on the way to the theatre and worked out a plan of action. Raquel had always been camera-wise, and she maneuvered herself into the line of stars where she knew she would be the closest to the photographers — in an unobstructed position where there would be no other arms, faces or heads in the way.

"She instinctively knew that it would be her picture which would be used in the papers," said Curtis. "Her dark skin on that white dress really made her stand out in that crowd.

"It was that picture, thanks to the London press, which 'made' Raquel an international celebrity — being photographed with the Queen of England. It didn't hurt her in the States, either. One of the wire services picked it up and it appeared in practically every major newspaper at home!"

Raquel Welch was on her way to becoming a major star, featured in over twenty pictures, including *Bandolero, 100 Rifles, The Oldest Profession, Bedazzled, The Beloved, Myra Breckinridge, Flare Up, Kansas City Bombers, Fuzz, Bluebeard, The Last of Sheila, The Three Musketeers, The Four Musketeers, The Wild Party, Mother Jugs & Speed* and *The Prince and the Pauper.*

Since she filed her law suit against MGM, she has appeared in one television movie, *The Legend of Walks Far Woman,* in 1984.

At the trial, Welch further testified that she had accepted the role of a hooker with the proverbial heart of gold for $250,000—most of which she forfeited when she was fired. She further stated it was because she saw it as her "big chance as an actress."

So eager was she to win the part that she even agreed to do a nude scene, despite the fact that she had refused other roles that demanded nudity—among them an offer from Begelman to star in the film version of Irving Wallace's *The Fan Club.* She had publicly referred to the film as a piece of sleaze.

Under cross examination, Welch admitted that she had requested a larger trailer/dressing room than the studio had provided and then requested alterations in the larger one to provide room for a professional makeup chair. While alterations were being made, she had, on two occasions, applied her own makeup at home. She added, however, that she had never been late for a set call during the six days she worked on the film prior to Michael Phillips' call.

In his opening statement, Welch's attorney Edward Mosk charged: "What we have here is a case about some very weak people, blaming someone else for their own inadequacies."

Mosk characterized director David Ward as an "inexperienced, not terribly competent, first time director" whose own job "was in danger." Mosk added that the $10 million movie was already $84,000 over budget by December 4th.

Mosk argued that Phillips' phone call to Raquel followed a December 16th memo from MGM's Chief Executive Officer Frank Rosenfelt to Begelman pointing out that the film was over budget.

The following day, according to Mosk, Begelman met with Phillips and David Chasman, a studio vice president. Shortly thereafter, Chasman contacted Debra Winger's manager to see whether she would be immediately available. Mosk promised to show that the filmmakers *conspired* to replace Raquel Welch even before the incidents in dispute occurred. Said Mosk: "David Begelman needed a scapegoat to protect himself from everyone!"

Ominously for MGM, Mosk added that, while Raquel Welch had earned $1.6 million for her film work in the six years preceding *Cannery Row,* "My client has not made one single film since."

The long arm of the oligarchy and the self-admitted forger and embezzler, David Begelman, had "reached out" to prevent her working again. Others in the past who had the temerity to file suit against a member of the oligarchy — a major Hollywood studio — had suffered the same fate.

MGM's attorney, Christina Snyder, referred to Raquel Welch as "a temperamental actress...who, if she could not have her own way, refused to talk to the producer, refused to talk to the director." She further countered that "the last thing they [MGM] wanted to do was to terminate Miss Welch, but she gave them no choice." Snyder, in our opinion from covering the trial, appeared to be in over her head in such a high profile case. She continued rambling in her opening remarks, stating that "the plaintiff refused to follow instructions," adding "when the going gets rough on every single motion picture Miss Welch has worked on, she falls back on the words: 'I was a scapegoat.'"

Raquel Welch has become embroiled with many people during her career, including co-stars — both male and female. But in entirely different types of situations from the stated ones for which MGM summarily fired her. One of her most publicized feuds revolved around *Myra Breckinridge* and the legendary Mae West. The feud probably erupted in the world press and gossip columns because of the controversial nature of the film itself.

Said Patrick Curtis: "It just so happened that Mae, as ancient as she was at the time, considered herself the star of the film, even though she was murdered by the critics after it was released."

The real blame for the feud lay at the feet of neo-phyte British director Michael Sarne. According to Curtis: "He was a miserable, sadistic bastard, in my opinion, who delighted in stirring things up between the performers.

"Robert Fryer, the producer, was a very weak man while making this film and it seemed he just could not cope with this headstrong, upstart young Englishman— a former actor in Cee minus British films, also known as "Quota Quickies"—making his first and last film in Hollywood."

We visited the set frequently. It made good copy because of the hype being generated by the film. It was in a constant state of turmoil because of the director, who felt, in his own sadistic way, that that was the atmosphere in which people worked best.

Raquel had been working every day for two or three weeks when Mae West made *le grande entrance* into the studio and onto the set—a scene not too unlike Gloria Swanson's studio scene in *Sunset Boulevard.*

"The first day she arrived," said Curtis, "Raquel sent her a huge bouquet of roses to try to smooth the way for both of them to work together; Mae was the sex symbol of the thirties, Raquel the symbol of the seventies.

"It didn't work."

As we later learned, Raquel erupted when she accidently learned that it was in Mae West's contract that no one in the film could wear black and white except her. Fryer, as producer, should have notified Welch, but, afraid of stirring up trouble, had not. He had also neglected to notify Theodore von Runkle.

Theodore, who had won an Oscar for the dress designs for *Bonnie and Clyde* a few years earlier, designed the wardrobe for *Myra Breckinridge*. One of the dresses was totally black with a white ruffle around the neck and sleeves. It was designed to be worn by Raquel in her first scene with Mae.

Sarne, continuing his sadistic trend, informed Mae that Raquel was wearing a black and white dress minutes before Welch was due on set. Mae made it clear she was not going to work if Raquel wore the dress. Raquel made it clear she was not going to work unless she did and went home.

Stand off!

When Raquel reported for work the next day so that she would not be placed on suspension, the dress was gone from her dressing room wardrobe.

"It had been 'confiscated' by Fryer," explained Curtis. "Raquel called him and told him — in no uncertain terms, because I was there at the time — 'That's the dress that everybody ok'd months ago and approved for the scene. It's a lovely dress and I'm going to wear it. I'm going home until it's returned or else Mae West can shove the dress and contract up her ass!'"

The dress was eventually returned because Welch refused to leave for the set until it was. Eventually, she agreed to the white portions of the dress being dyed a very light blue. It photographed almost pure white. Mae West was appeased and Raquel got her way.

But Raquel had not instigated the trouble. A very weak producer and an incompetent director created a problem which could have been avoided before shooting had even begun.

Raquel could hardly be faulted.

On her second day on the stand, Raquel testified that, when she had learned she had been fired from *Cannery Row,* "It was devastating to me. I was in a state of shock and sort of felt my professional life was over. I was left with the feeling that after all the years—fifteen or sixteen—I had worked to establish myself, it was finished; it was over with. I was not wanted as part of the movie making community."

MGM had refused to pay her the balance due on her $250,000 pay-or-play contract, of which she had received just $54,000 for the two weeks she had completed on the film. "I believe they fired me so that they would not have to pay me," she testified tearfully.

Under questioning from her attorney, she continued: "I did not get offered any roles in any movies for a long time." Parts she was eventually offered, she continued, included a Nazi and a vampire—both of which she refused. The "Old Boy Network" had presented a solid front: if one was being sued by her, the others would not hire her.

Snyder attempted to demonstrate—under cross examination—that Welch was temperamental and that her career was not hurt by the firing. Raquel admitted that she made as much as $30,000 per week during her six-month run in Broadway's *Woman of the Year* and that additional income from her beauty book, video cassette and commercial endorsements totaled more than $3 million since 1980 — nearly twice the income she had earned as a film actress in the six years preceding *Cannery Row.*

Questioned about her professional behavior on earlier projects, Welch admitted refusing to re-shoot a scene in *The Wild Party* a few years earlier when the director found it boring. "He thought it was boring because I had my clothes on. He wanted me to take them off!" she added.

The conspiracy aspect on which the case was to turn, however, had not yet come out in the testimony.

Raquel Welch was fated to be publicized in the gossip columns and fan magazines as being hard to get along with because of the *Myra Breckinridge* incident and several which occurred during the filming of *100 Rifles.*

According to her ex-husband, "She is a very demanding woman and knows what she wants. She generally gets it by fair means or foul!"

101 Rifles was one of Welch's seven pictures under her contract with 20th Century-Fox. She was co-starred with Burt Reynolds, with whom she had no problem at the time.

"Let's face it," said Curtis, "Burt at the time was just another journeyman actor and not in a position to feud with anyone. It was in *Fuzz* several years later that he and Raquel got into it — thanks to him and his vapid remarks."

Burly Jim Brown, a former Cleveland Browns football great, was just beginning his start in films. He had been approved by Raquel for the picture.

Brown, however, in those early days, had a reputation for throwing girls out of windows and off balconies. Just before he left for location, his latest girl friend had suffered a well-publicized plunge off the second floor balcony of Brown's West Hollywood apartment. After a stretch in the hospital, she joined him in Almeria.

"This was Brown's first film outside the United States," explained Curtis, "and it all started when we arrived at the Madrid airport. Because of other films shooting in Spain at the time, there were hundreds of photographers milling around and we had incredible problems.

"But, again, Raquel, with that intuitive sense of design to be in the front row of everything—especially around cameras—was the center of attention. Reynolds and Jim Brown stepped off the plane behind us and were completely ignored by the photographers, even though they knew they were featured in the film. The lensers had been well briefed by the publicist on the film before we arrived."

According to Curtis's recollection, Brown was really "pissed off about that. Being ignored by the press, he declined our invitation to join us on our private charter for the flight south to Almeria. After that, things went from bad to worse between he and Raquel. On the other hand, Burt accepted our invitation and came with us on the flight and everything was okay between us.

"While shooting the film, all Jim Brown would talk about was Black Power...and all that palaver for ten or twelve weeks," said Curtis. "Who needs eight to ten hours a day of political and racial dissertations?

"Raquel completely ignored him...so much so that he really was getting more annoyed with her every day."

When we were among reporters visiting the set in Almeria, we noticed that Brown used to stand behind the camera, a building, or anything else handy during his off-camera dialogue and spit at Raquel. This was not the type of conduct to endear yourself to your co-worker.

When we tried to get publicity stills of Raquel with Brown, she refused to pose with him, even though she was required to under the terms of her contract. Although not the instigator of the problem, she bore the brunt and the bad publicity.

As the trial came to a close, Raquel was asked about her demands for a larger trailer on *Cannery Row* and was shown a photograph by Snyder of the type of 32 foot mobile home that had been provided for her. Welch replied, "It was certainly a very attractive mobile home, but it had practical problems because it was very narrow; it was very cramped."

Sensing the case was slipping away from her, Snyder tried to draw in a personality conflict between Raquel and producer Michael Phillips, asking her why she had refused to speak to him during the weekend in which she was fired. The actress replied, "He had lied to me. I didn't feel like I could talk to him in a coherent way on that weekend."

For four weeks, Mosk argued that MGM, Begelman, Phillips and director David Ward made Welch the scapegoat on *Cannery Row* when it began to run over budget, forcing her firing so that she could be replaced by Debra Winger.

Barry Hirsch, a powerful entertainment lawyer, testified under cross examination that he had negotiated a deal for Debra Winger days *before* Raquel Welch was fired.

This was the "conspiracy" Christina Snyder tried to play down during the trial. She — and the studio — knew the case would turn on it. They had negotiated with another actress prior to firing Raquel Welch. This, under California law, constituted conspiracy. Welch claimed that Winger was hired with the cost overrun on the picture approaching $100,000. By signing Winger for a lot less and inventing the "makeup at home" controversy, the studio hoped to evade paying Welch the $194,000 due on her contract.

After three days of deliberation, a Superior Court jury ruled in favor of the actress on all four counts in her multi-million dollar law suit. The studio was found to have breached her contract when she was fired. As the court clerk read the amount of damages totalling more than $10.8 million, Raquel Welch took a deep, slow breath, leaned back in her chair and raised her arms above her head like a victorious fighter. She then dissolved into tears and embraced Edward Mosk.

"I never expected such an overwhelming victory as this," said a tearful Welch outside the courtroom.

"I think that what this shows is that it's important to stand up for your rights, and I hope that women in and out of Hollywood stand up for their rights when they feel they've been wronged."

According to one juror, "All the facts pointed to breach of contract by the studio — and a conspiracy."

This is why the studio was assessed for most of the $7,650,000 of the punitive damages; Phillips was levied $694,444, Begelman, $27,500. No judgement was levied against Ward and the studio was ordered to pay the balance of her salary, $194,000. There was an assessment of $450,000 for defamation of character and another $2.1 million for loss of earnings.

In an interview a few days after the trial, Raquel added, "I also think that perhaps this comes at a time when you're seeing the end of a kind of era in Hollywood...where a lot of unscrupulous behavior has been condoned (in the past) and now we're on the horizon of much better times."

A chastened defense attorney defended her loss and pointed out, rather lamely, that Raquel Welch had "only" received half of what she had sought in the original suit. "We believe we will prevail in the appeals process..."

MGM did not "prevail in the appeals process" and finally settled the suit, with interest, for close to $15 million dollars.

But it was a empty victory for Raquel Welch. Her "better times" never came. She has never made another picture in Hollywood; nor, unfortunately, is she ever likely to.

That's the way it works in Hollywood; sue the studios and never work again.

CHAPTER FOUR

Two Bizarre and Unexplained Deaths

*"I believe David Whiting was murdered and
it was covered up by a powerful
Hollywood conspiracy."*
— **Forest Hinderliter**
Gila Bend, AZ Detective (Ret.)

THE MAN WHO DIED DURING
CAT DANCING

Two Hollywood deaths certainly rank high in the realm of "mysterious," "bizarre" or "unsolved." One was the death of David Whiting, manager of British actress Sarah Miles, during the filming of *The Man Who Loved Cat Dancing.* The other was the death of the well known "heavy" Steve Cochran.

In February, 1973, Metro-Goldwyn-Mayer dispatched a company of actors and technicians to Arizona to start shooting *The Man Who Loved Cat Dancing,* a western starring Sarah Miles, Burt Reynolds, the late Lee J. Cobb, George Hamilton, Jack Warden and Jay Silverheels.

The detective who originally questioned Reynolds, Miles and others about the body of David Whiting found in the actress' room, today says, almost twenty years later, "it was murder." Both he and the coroner who examined the corpse accuse Hollywood bigwigs of covering up the crime.

The now ex-coroner Milford Winsor said, in 1987, that he had a letter alleging that Whiting's death was connected to a passionate love triangle involving Reynolds, Miles and the dead man. The letter was not brought out during the investigation because it was unsigned.

The morning following the death, we flew to Tucson with a photographer to cover the story. The plane was filled with members of the legal staff of MGM and ten other reporters. Also on board were MGM CEO Frank Rosenfelt and Reynold's press agent, David Gershenson. Because of Rosenfelt's presence, most veteran reporters instinctively realized that this would be a high profile case with plenty to cover up. Seldom would a CEO of a major studio involve himself in the death of an employee or an MGM star unless there was something to cover up.

The death of Britisher David Whiting would create a scandal in Britain, but receive scant attention in the Los Angeles press.

Sarah Miles first arrived in Hollywood in 1970 on a publicity tour for David Lean's long-in-the-making *Ryan's Daughter,* which also starred Robert Mitchum, the late Trevor Howard, John Mills and Leo

("Rumpole") McKern. She was then married to Robert Bolt, the playwright who had authored the screenplays of *Lawrence of Arabia* and *A Man For All Seasons,* and who had adapted the screenplay of *Ryan's Daughter* for director David Lean.

On her first afternoon, she had two appointments arranged by the MGM publicity department. The first was with a *Time* magazine correspondent at noon; the next with a *Vogue* photographer at 3:30 p.m. The latter appointment worried her considerably. *Vogue* wanted to feature her as one of the three most beautiful women in the world and there — on her left cheek — was a boil!

Miles was not in a particularly cooperative spirit. Nor did her mood improve when the *Time* correspondent arrived — a half hour late.

According to her later recollections, David Whiting tried to keep memories of the British Empire alive by wearing a well cut, three-piece English suit and a very proper Turnbull & Asser shirt. He carried a gold Dunhill lighter and Dunhill cigarettes in their traditional red and gold box. He also carried a bottle which he claimed was his own personal Bloody Mary mix.

After discussing the boil on Sarah's cheek, Whiting claimed he knew the best dermatologist in Beverly Hills and a perfect antidote. After taking it, Miles' boil subsided enough so that she could pose for the *Vogue* layout.

Miles was grateful and intrigued by Whiting's British pomposity and intelligence. When he asked if they could meet again for a further interview the following evening, she agreed.

But Miles was becoming more and more disenchanted. When MGM promised her she would have her long awaited work permit in time for her appearances on the Manhattan morning network television shows, she decided to leave for New York immediately. While she was waiting for her flight in the TWA Ambassadors Club, she was surprised by Whiting, who announced that he was taking the same flight and had secured the seat next to her. The next morning, he showed up in her suite at the Sherry-Netherland. He had taken a room on the same floor. Miles claimed she never encouraged him; she obviously never told him to disappear, either.

Miles' work permit had become a problem. As a small army of press agents from MGM and an outside agency traipsed in and out of her suite, reporting delays and failures, Sarah — in language she must have learned on the London docks — berated them. She informed them it was a complete waste of her time and MGM's money for her to hang around awaiting a mythical work permit.

It was then that David Whiting became involved. One telephone call to an unknown entity in the bowels of the United States bureaucracy in New York and her work permit arrived by messenger within a hour. She, and MGM, were impressed.

MGM employed Whiting as Miles' press agent, personal manager and general factotum. Pleasant enough company at first, he eventually came to live with Miles and Bolt in their country home in England. He accompanied her on all her travels, but slowly became somewhat of an embarrassment to the couple.

They asked him to leave, but Whiting threatened to commit suicide if he was forced to leave Sarah. In March, 1972, he was admitted to a London hospital after taking an overdose. The Bolts reluctantly kept him on and he journeyed to the United States with Sarah for *Cat Dancing*. Because of prior commitments, Bolt remained behind in England. Sarah also brought her son, Thomas, along with his nanny.

Whiting's body was found in Sarah Miles' room at the TraveLodge in Gila Bend, Arizona, after a night of intense partying to celebrate Reynold's 38th birthday.

A hastily convened coroner's inquest decided that Whiting had died of a drug overdose, but did not rule whether it was an accident, suicide—or murder.

Sergeant Forrester Hinderliter of the Gila Bend police force was the first official on the scene. As he stepped out of his patrol car, an MGM official who had been on the Western Air Lines flight with us, talked to him in confidence.

We were later told that Hinderliter had been told that Whiting had been drinking, had swallowed a lot of pills, and was dead. This was the story we dutifully reported to our London newspaper and European press service.

Both Hinderliter and Milford Winsor, the coroner who conducted the inquest, claim the circumstances surrounding Whiting's death were covered up by "a powerful Hollywood conspiracy." Both now admit that they allowed the fast talking "Hollywood attorneys" to intimidate them and that key evidence was overlooked.

They also claim stories were changed mid-investigation after careful coaching by the same attorneys.

When Hinderliter found the male body in Miles' room, it had no pulse. Pale blotches on the hands, neck and forehead indicated that death had come several hours before it was discovered at around lunchtime, 12:30 p.m. The man was lying on his back on the floor of a partitioned "dressing room" area of Room 127. About a dozen capsules were beside the body, many of them in groups of two or three as though they had been carefully placed there. Later, Burt Reynolds would testify that he had seen pills on top of the dead man's arm when the body was discovered. No one explained how they got there.

Hinderliter wondered how the man had come to collapse and die in what was clearly a woman's bedroom. The dresser was full of cosmetics and, as was usual in film locations, a woman's wardrobe hung on hangers around the room. A hair piece was draped across a vinyl chair.

Hinderliter then asked for the man's name and position with the company. He was told "in an almost conspiratorial tone" that his name had been David Whiting and "he was Sarah Miles' business manager. He was found dead in her room." He was told that Miles was in producer Martin Poll's room, but that she was "much too upset to talk. She's had a terrible experience."

Upset or not, Hinderliter wanted to see her. After questioning Miles for several minutes, he recounted that the actress told him, "He was my business manager, but all he wanted to do was fuck me all the time and I wasn't going to be fucked by him." Sarah Miles had never been one to mince words; it was one of the reasons she was favorite 'copy' for the London tabloids.

The pills had indicated that Whiting died of an overdose. But, when the coroner arrived from a shooting death on the other side of town, he and Hinderliter turned over the body, revealing a bloody, star-shaped wound on the back of the head. As the body rested partially on the tile floor of the bathroom, blood started to seep from the wound.

At the inquest later, the autopsy doctor would explain that the star-shaped contusion was one inch in diameter at the back of the head, to the right of the occipital point, "the kind of wound we frequently see in people who fall on the back of the head."

"This, of course, does not preclude the possibility of the decedent having been pushed," he added ominously. He also testified, when queried, that additional "scratches" and "contused abrasions" on the lower abdomen, and multiple hemorrhages — bruises — on the chest and the left shoulder "would be consistent with someone having been in a scuffle or a fight."

But, despite the suggestive marks on the outside of Whiting's torso, the cause of death, he concluded, was to be found elsewhere.

When officials checked Whiting's room, Number 119, they found bloodstains on a pillow, a bath towel, tissue and a room key — the key to Sarah Miles' room.

This was not the first time that Sarah Miles had dealt with death around her—death involving people whom she knew very well.

"There was one woman and one homosexual. The woman was a school friend of mine who brought her little boy and came to live with me and then wouldn't leave. My husband finally said, 'This is ridiculous; she has to go.'

"I told him I couldn't tell her," she revealed in an interview several years following the Whiting affair. "My husband finally told her it was no longer possible to support her. She left the next day—and jumped off a building."

The school friend, an unsuccessful actress, had recently been discharged from a mental home and had reclaimed her son from relatives. But Sarah Miles waved that away as just another person's life in which she had become hopelessly involved—as she had Whiting's.

The man was a landscape gardener, John Windeatt, living in the gardener's cottage on their property. He had not paid rent for two years and owed the Bolts $3,500. "He didn't give any reason for putting his head in a gas oven and committing suicide. Rather silly, I thought," was Miles' reaction.

After the discovery of the items in Whiting's room, Hinderliter questioned Miles and Reynolds together in Reynold's room.

"Burt Reynolds, bare chested and wearing skin tight leather pants, began consoling Miss Miles," Hinderliter later recalled.

"One of them — I can't remember which — told me that *there had been a scuffle between Reynolds and Whiting in Reynold's room.*

"He'd pushed Whiting, who fell and hit his head on a coffee table. That's as far as we got in the interview. At that moment, the door burst open and in came two or three Hollywood film types in jeans and Gucci loafers. They began hugging and kissing Burt."

According to Hinderliter, Miles said that she had been to a birthday party for Reynolds the night before in another desert town about forty miles away. She left early and drove back with Lee J. Cobb, who wanted to show off his new car — a Maserati.

She had danced and drank in the motel lounge until midnight. Later, she went to Reynold's room to apologize for leaving his party.

Hinderliter said Miles told him that when she returned to her own room around 3 a.m. Whiting jumped out at her from a closet. He demanded to know where she had been and slapped her when she refused to account for her movements. She had then sent for Reynolds who took her back to his room, where she spent the night.

The next morning, sometime between 8 and 10 a.m., she returned to her own room and found Whiting's body. She hurried back to Reynold's room to tell Burt.

The studio had been contacted immediately by producer Martin Poll. It was almost noon before the police were notified.

Then came the three ring circus of an inquest.

Miles testified that Whiting had given her a nasty beating after he jumped out at her, but Hinderliter testified that he had noticed no bruises or marks of any kind to indicate that such a beating had taken place. "I was virtually called a liar by Reynolds and Sarah Miles with their evidence," Hinderliter said later.

At the inquest, Hinderliter now indicates, questioning revolved around how many pills Whiting had taken and the pills Reynolds said he "saw" on or around the body after he had been summoned by Miles.

"The jury decided that he had taken enough to kill him even though experts disagreed on that point including the autopsy doctor," recounts Hinderliter.

Meantime, MGM attorneys obtained an injunction from a Phoenix judge preventing any further testimony by Reynolds and Miles at the inquest. The studio claimed they were needed for work on the film.

No one attempted to explain — or even mentioned — the head injury or the blood. "There were just too many unanswered questions."

Among the "unanswered questions" — and one which bore the prudence of MGM's injunction — was the amount of prescription drugs and over-the-counter medications found in Miles' room. The Arizona State Police reported there were multi-vitamins, several antibiotics including Ampicillin and Serax Oxasepan for the treatment of anxiety and depression. Also catalogued were capsules of Dalmane, a hypnotic and some other unidentified capsules.

The wound on the back of Whiting's head has never been explained. An MGM lawyer made an attempt to explain it by suggesting that David Whiting simply smashed the back of his head against a wall in a fit of rage or a drugged stupor.

Another "unanswered question" was an item missing from the scene. Burt Reynolds had told Hinderliter that, when he was summoned "to view the body," he had noticed a pill bottle clenched in one of Whiting's closed fists. He then rushed back and asked Sarah if she knew what the pills were. "She was too upset or distraught to reply," she told the sergeant.

The pill box had disappeared — conveniently or otherwise. Reynolds could not remember what he had done with it. He might have had it in his hand when he returned a few minutes later to the death scene. He did remember seeing a prescription-type label of some sort.

The pill box was never found.

Could it have contained the capsules found on top of Whiting's body and on the floor beside him? No one has ever been able — or wanted — to explain the pills on the body. It is possible the deceased could have knocked some pills onto the floor and onto his own arm and body while lying curled up on the floor — but not very likely.

No one involved in the death of David Whiting has admitted knowing anything about them.

"I believe some pills could have been forced down the throat of Whiting when he was dazed or semi-conscious after striking his head. I called it murder then, and I call it murder today," said Hinderliter in 1987, as he stressed that Miles and Reynolds both changed the stories they had originally told him.

"The Hollywood crowd had taken over a small town in the desert and used it and its people to suit their own ends. I was convinced that an attempt at a cover-up was being made. There hasn't been a day gone by in all the intervening yearsthat I haven't thought about it," he recalls.

The coroner, Winsor, also feels the "high powered" Hollywood lawyers dazzled the jury of local people that he had called out of a local coffee shop while they were having lunch. He had asked them to view the body as a coroner's jury is required to do under Arizona law.

"At the time, I certainly didn't think it was suicide," he adds to the Hinderliter analysis. "And I'm not convinced that Whiting took an 'accidental' overdose, either.

"The investigation had hardly gotten started when those Hollywood types arrived by the dozen. Every one clammed up and left town immediately for the Rio Rico Inn in Nogales — over 150 miles away."

The coroner also complained that there was too much delay — as long as four hours — before the police were notified — Miss Miles having changed her story more than once about what time she discovered Whiting's body. She had obviously been well coached.

"Neither Burt Reynolds nor Sarah Miles were asked about the injuries or what they had originally told Sergeant Hinderliter. I felt I was under a great deal of pressure."

Winsor said that the case has troubled him ever since.

David Gershenson states that his client, Burt Reynolds, was "satisfied with the findings of the coroner," and, as far as he was concerned, the case was finished years ago. But, over the years, many have suggested that David Whiting was literally "star struck" that night — and that Reynolds was the star.

Burt Reynolds has always had a reputation in Hollywood for an explosive temper and an itch to fight.

In 1986, Reynolds punched out director Dick Richards in Las Vegas and had to be held back by a stuntman after tensions exploded on the set of *Heat,* the film that — it was hoped — would put Reynolds back on top of the box office heap. It didn't.

Even though it was written by William Goldman, one of Hollywood's top screen writers, *Heat* was a bomb, following on the heels of *Cannonball II, Stick* and *City Heat.*

Nor is Reynold's particularly tactful about his leading ladies.

In 1988, he was enlisted to co-star with Kathleen Turner in yet another remake of *The Front Page* — *Switching Channels* — when Michael Caine was tied up on *Jaws 4* and couldn't be released in time. The film also starred Christopher Reeve.

Turner and Reynolds argued constantly during shooting and for sometime after the film was completed. Reynolds eventually stated that working on the film was so traumatic that the sight of his co-star made him sick.

"When I see Kathleen Turner, I get physically ill,"

said Reynolds. "If we seemed to get along well on screen, it's damn good acting. *Switching Channels* was not my favorite film," he attested to a London newspaper reporter.

While he was working on *The Man Who Loved Cat Dancing* around Gila Bend, he regaled the locals with tales of his past fights, but added that he'd decided to leave that part of his life behind him.

However, if Reynolds, as rumors persist, had lost control of himself and given Whiting a beating, it seems more than likely that the body would have shown more evidence than it did in the autopsy. There was no evidence on the walls or anywhere else that Whiting had either fallen or been thrown against them hard enough to create the wound on his head. On the other hand, the parking lot outside the rooms was asphalt. A beating or fall could have occurred there and all evidence been washed away by the sharp Sunday morning rain that had inundated Gila Bend.

The verbal evidence given by those involved is what thoroughly confused the issue for the police and the coroner. Even the testimony of Thomas' nanny was confusing. She said that she awoke at seven-thirty and was very cold. She walked through the connecting door into Sarah's room and discovered the outside door wide open to the rain. She shut it and headed back for the inner door and into her own and the child's room. She said that she never saw the body in the course of her trip.

When Hinderliter saw the body at 12:30 or thereabouts, he found Whiting's legs sticking out beyond the end of the dressing room partition. Returning to her own room, the nanny was walking toward the end of the dressing room partition. One must surmise that she was walking directly toward the protruding body of David Whiting.

Although the lights were still on, the nanny testified that she was drowsy and saw no body.

Several possibilities exist: either the body was not there; the body was there and the nanny did not, in fact, see it; or the body was there—dead or alive—the nanny spotted it, figured the person was drunk or passed out, and went back to bed without reporting it.

She could also have reported it to someone who waited four hours before reporting it to the police.

Hinderliter told us, recalling the interviews with Miles, that she said she went back to her room around eight o'clock in the morning. She later said ten o'clock.

"I didn't push it at the time because she was so upset. At the time, I was just working on the theory of a drug overdose."

Eleven days later, in tapes recorded at the Rio Rico Inn, Sarah said it was around eleven fifteen when she returned to her room and found the body!

Obviously, everyone involved was playing it by ear and changing their stories to fit whatever the attorneys told them to say.

And there it stands today—almost twenty years later. Perhaps it was an accident, or a drug overdose or, possibly, an unexplained murder as officials in Gila Bend still insist. No one will ever know. All the lies that were told—under oath—at the inquest accomplished only a bizarre confusion about the cause of the death of David Whiting.

His death was deeply felt by all.

The afternoon of the death, the local funeral director was in Room 127 with the body of David Whiting, which had been released by the coroner. Sarah Miles sent her nanny to tell them she wanted to get into the room to get a dress—because they were having a party in the bar and she wanted to get up there.

Burt Reynolds was also due at a party at the local Elks Club in honor of his birthday. The actor discussed whether it would be "proper" to attend. The party was for him, of course, and he would disappoint a lot of local people if he didn't appear.

Reynolds said that if the death was an accident, then it was tragic and no time to attend a party. However, since MGM had decided it was suicide, then this guy was so worthless he didn't have the guts to face life. Why spoil the party?

Reynolds went and was the life of the party!

Traveling to Tucson that day, all of us aboard the Western Airlines flight sensed that more than a "drug overdose" had killed Sarah Miles' business manager—the original flash on the Associated Press wire from its stringer on the local paper in Gila Bend.

Most of us, in retrospect, still feel the same way

"Mr. Cochran finally stopped complaining.
He let out a deep sigh, opened his eyes,
and then he no longer complained."
— **Lorenza Infanta**
A Female Crew Member Aboard
Actor Steve Cochran's Yacht
Rogue

DEATH ON THE HIGH SEAS
The Bizarre and Unexplained
Death of Steve Cochran

Described in several film reference books as "an American leading man, usually a good looking 'heavy,'" Steve Cochran spent a great deal of time in courtrooms in and around Los Angeles. In May of 1953, boxer Lenwood "Buddy" Wright was awarded $16,500 after suing Cochran for $405,000 in damages for swatting him over the head with a baseball bat at a New Year's Eve party.

Again in 1953, Cochran was the target of police gunfire during a five mile traffic chase through the

Culver City streets abutting MGM studios. Driving a Porsche, he refused to stop for a police car with red lights and siren. Officer Roger Deveaux had to fire a shot in the air in order to get Cochran to pull over.

Two years later, Cochran was arrested on a civil court order in Durban, South Africa, accusing him of adultery with jockey Arthur Cecil Miller's wife. The terms of the order provided for 30 days to institute action against Cochran, who was in South Africa making *Mozambique,* in which the jockey's wife has a small part. Cochran was accused of spending several nights with Heather Miller in a Durban hotel where the film company was based.

The charges were eventually dropped when Miller's wife sued for divorce and Cochran left for Germany to star in *The Deadly Companions.*

In August, 1960, Cochran's 40-foot schooner sailed into the Los Angeles breakwater in fog and sank in more than 30 feet of water. Cochran, two young women, a miniature chimpanzee and two dogs scrambled to safety on the breakwater.

Cochran said that the engine in the $16,000 vessel had failed while he was returning home from South Catalina Island and he was at the helm about dawn in a dense fog under sail when the accident occurred. The flight of a sea gull had alerted him that land must be close and he had put the helm hard over, but it was too late. "I couldn't see the rocks until we were on them," he later explained.

Hedy Graaberg, 19, climbed out on the bowsprit and jumped to the rocks. Nicole Makay of Hollywood, also 19, swam to safety with the chimp around her neck. Cochran threw the dogs into the sea and they swam to the breakwater, while he climbed to the rocks.

After making *Carnival Story* for the King Brothers, Cochran became interested in working in Europe on a steady basis. He starred or co-starred in many Italian films, and then returned to Hollywood to be featured in many early television films, including *Highway Patrol.*

In the winter of 1964, Cochran sailed from San Pedro in his 40-foot schooner, *The Rogue,* which he had purchased in Mexico earlier that year. Aboard was an all-female crew. The trip was viewed by many as a publicity stunt. Reportedly, Cochran was going to make arrangements to film an independent production, *Capt. O'Flynn,* off Guatemala.

The wire services reported that the all-female crew left the expedition in Ensenada and that Cochran sailed alone to Acapulco. He advertised for another all-girl crew in a local newspaper, and three young females, all friends, applied. The three were on board *The Rogue* when it was intercepted off the port of Champerico in Guatemala by the Coast Guard on June 27, 1965.

Cochran was found dead on the floundering schooner by the boarding party. A passing fishing trawler, anxious to return to port with its catch, had notified the naval authorities by radio of a derelict — or what appeared to be a vessel in distress.

Lorenza Infante de la Rosa, 14, Eva Montero Castellanos, 19, and Eugenia Bautista, 25, told the coast guard that they had set out from Acapulco and drifted to where they were found. The schooner was towed to Champerico and the women were placed in custody prior to questioning.

Born in Eureka, California, Steve Cochran's real name was Robert Alexander Cochran. He grew up in Wyoming and attended the University of Wyoming. He received his acting experience at the Federal Arts Theatre in Detroit and served in the United States Army Special Services during World War II.

A Warner Bros. scout spotted him in *Diamond Lil* on Broadway and he was placed under contract for Warner Bros., appearing in *The Chase, The Damned Don't Cry, Highway 301* and *The Tanks Are Coming.*

In the late 1940s, he tired of such fare and sought release from his contract. He acquired a script, *Come Next Spring,* and sold himself and the property to Republic Pictures, starring with another Warner Bros. cast off, Ann Sheridan. One critic described the film: "This is a D.W. Griffith pastoral melodrama which surprisingly works pretty well and leaves one with the intended warm glow."

Despite his many years of activity, Hollywood knew very little about Cochran. One reason was that he seldom mixed in Hollywood society or social events. He was offered several other films as a result of the success of *Come Next Spring.* He turned them down in favor of a nomadic life.

In 1963, a film in which he starred with Merle Oberon in Mexico, *Of Love and Desire,* produced by

Victor Stofoll for New World Pictures, opened on Broadway without the film colony—either in Hollywood or New York—even being aware he had made it. Following the opening, it was described in several reviews as an "unwise, sensationalist vehicle for an aging leading lady." It closed almost as fast as it had opened.

In an interview at Sardi's following the film's inauspicious opening, Cochran switched attention to another film and dismissed the Oberon film as "nothing really. But I recently finished producing and playing the lead in a picture I made in the Bahamas, *Tell Me In The Sunlight,* written by an unknown writer, Jo Helms. My leading lady was Shary Marshall—and she's an unknown—but she won't be when this one is released." The film was never released.

Cochran is best remembered as Hollywood's quintessential "heavy" for Warner Bros. in *The Damned Don't Cry,* with Joan Crawford, and *I, Mobster.* He is also remembered for his role as the drunkard who returns to his home town and finally gains respect in *Come Next Spring.*

According to Guatemalen authorities, a "mysterious ailment" paralyzed Cochran before he died in the schooner. The three female crew members told the Coast Guard authorities that he died on June 15, 1965, leaving them helpless at sea in a boat they could not sail. They had been adrift with the body for twelve days before being found and towed into Champerico. Cochran was paying them 90 pesos a day (about $17 in

1965), but had promised them more "when the filming started."

In an interview with United Press International following their ordeal, the three said Cochran struggled against a hurricane at the helm of the schooner for two days and two nights before he died. He had taught them elementary steering, but had taken the helm of the 40-foot vessel when it became necessary during the storm. "His death was very frightening. He died almost in the arms of Lorenza, who had been bathing his fevered face with a wet towel," said Eva Montero Castellanos, adding that Cochran fought high winds and huge waves by himself when the vessel ran into the storm off the coast of Oaxaca. She added that he was "completely exhausted and very sick when it was over," and became delirious. But there was no medicine on board with which to treat him.

Infante added, "Mr. Cochran finally stopped complaining of the pain. He let out a deep sigh, opened his eyes and no longer complained."

Hollywood actress Julie Gambol told the *Los Angeles Times*—upon hearing of Cochran's death—that she had accompanied Cochran and a Spanish teacher to Ensenada. "He was teaching me sailing and the Spanish language for my part in the *Capt. O'Flynn* movie," the 21-year-old, auburn-haired Gambol related. "He was training me so I could train other girls for their roles in the film."

Gambol added that she had planned to join Cochran in Costa Rica after he had signed the rest of the cast and crew required for the film.

The preliminary autopsy report showed that Cochran *may* have died of a "swelling of the lung." The cause of the swelling was unknown. The cause of death was officially attributed to acute infectious edema.

The crew members said Cochran told them he hoped to reach Costa Rica in eight or nine days where he was to meet a film crew and start filming. Following his death, the film crew was never located to confirm the story.

De la Rosa said the forward mast was damaged in another, lighter storm before the hurricane and this had slowed them down considerably. On June 14, the actor complained of severe headaches and fainting spells and soon became paralyzed. His temperature rose and he died shortly after 5:00 a.m. on the 15th.

When the Coast Guard towed the schooner into port, Cochran's body, following 12 days at sea, was found to be badly decomposed. At the time, the Guatemalan Medical Examiner, Dr. Abel Giron, told us by telephone—in halting English—that he knew Cochran personally and the body on which he performed the autopsy was the actor's. Although it had been difficult to identify, they had met previously, said Giron, on one of Cochran's visits to Guatemala searching for exotic locations in which to film.

The American consul in the port city said an American passport bearing the name Robert Alexander Cochran was found on the body, which was placed in a plain pine coffin and sent to Guatemala City to await instructions from Cochran's next of kin.

No sooner had the actor's body been flown to San Francisco for funeral services than his estranged third wife, Jonna Jensen Cochran, a 23-year old Beverly Hills secretary, sought to be named administrator of his estate—which, at the time, was believed to be more than $160,000. It was later discovered that $100,000 had been transferred to Cochran's 85-year-old mother several months before. Another survivor, daughter Xandria Johns, 23, of Centralia, Washington, also filed a claim. Prior to his death, Cochran told several friends—and his about-to-be ex-wife, Jonna—that his daughter had left home at the age of 16 and he had not heard from her in over five years. Cochran's will could not be located.

In October of 1965, a Santa Monica judge ruled that Jonna Cochran be granted one half of a $25,000 estate. It had come out in court testimony that Cochran had kept her a virtual prisoner in their rented San Fernando Valley home, never allowing her to travel more than ten miles from the house. She also testified that Cochran repeatedly told her that he would send her back to Denmark and told her, "I'm going to keep you and treat you this way because I do not want you to become Americanized." The judge ruled that an agreement waiving her claim to any part of Cochran's estate was obtained under duress.

Cochran's daughter received the other half of his $25,000 estate. It could not be proven that Cochran had surrendered $100,000 to his mother for any other purpose than as a gift and that she was entitled to keep the money.

It would appear that Cochran was attempting to live out his reel roles in real life. He never found a niche in either his native land or chosen profession — at which he was very good — and died on foreign soil or, perhaps one should say, on foreign waters.

Perhaps he preferred it that way.

CHAPTER FIVE

Oscar's Dirty Little Secrets

*"The Oscars are handed out by the self styled,
so-called Academy of Motion Picture Arts
& Sciences, which has little science
and even less art . . ."*
— **Ezra Goodman**
*The Fifty Year Decline & Fall
of Hollywood,* 1957

"Lord, how we honor ourselves . . ."
— **Rod Serling** *Twilight Zone*

One of the most bizarre rituals, rites of
passage and vicious exploitations of Hollywood is the
annual Oscar Derby—Hollywood's pat on the back to
itself—that occurs on a Monday in late March or early
April. Originally, Monday night was selected for
televising the event because that day is, traditionally, a
slow night at movie box offices.

In our thirty odd years of covering Hollywood
(and 20 of the annual events), many people outside of
the industry have inquired as to how the nominees (and
eventual winners) are selected. They also posed the
query: "Are they fixed?"

The number of Academy voters as of the fall of 1991 totaled 4,940 give or take a dozen or so, and all the competing interests argue against any effective conspiracy to fix the Oscars. But, stories persist that they can, at the very least, be manipulated.

Prior to the break up of the major studios, the number of votes for a nominee depended upon the number of Academy members employed by a particular studio at nomination time. A large number of Academy members looking for a job at that time suddenly found themselves hired by studios with particular projects to push through the nomination process. More recently, talent agencies and public relations firms in particular have exercised influence in the voting process.

We know of one actress—who usually receives "above the title" billing—who swears that one of the largest, most powerful agencies promised her an Oscar if she left the agent who had nurtured her and signed with them. Indignant, she turned down the obvious bribe.

"How can you promise that?" she asked. To which the agent trying to sign her replied, "We strongly suggest how our clients—who are members of the Academy—should vote. We tell our clients how to vote and we keep them working." Obviously, new clients are urged to apply for membership upon signing with the agency and a member-sponsor is immediately located.

When the top management at the largest agency in the industry won over Dan Aykroyd as a client from his manager of many years, they reportedly promised to deliver him a nomination—if not an Oscar itself.

Aykroyd landed the role of "Boolie" in *Driving Miss Daisy* and received a supporting actor nomination, but not the brass ring.

Producer Menachem Golan told us in Cannes recently that he had spent several hundred thousand dollars in a futile attempt to secure a nomination for his Cannon film's *The Runaway Train* in 1986. Jon Voight had already been awarded a Golden Globe as Best Actor for his compelling work in the film. Voight received an Oscar nomination, but no statuette. Golan's thousands had gone down the drain!

Why?

"When people ask me if the Oscars are honest, I say 'Yes' in terms of no one is actually cheating," said Golan.

"But it is *not* honest in terms of voting for the best movies. Of the over 4,000 people in the Academy, how many are salaried by the major companies—not studios, per se—or are under contract to the major agencies such as Creative Artists and Creative Management Associates? At least 2,500? 2,700? Maybe more."

Golan swears that voters with major companies, studios or agency affiliations stack the deck against the independent producers in two ways when the nominating process begins in January:

a. By voting for "house" product only as their first choice in the nomination process.

b. By ignoring those possibilities they consider the strongest competition.

Since every member can list five nominations for each category, but is not required to do so, this becomes a perfect method for stacking the deck. Only those members in each category—such as acting, writing, music or set decoration—can nominate in their category. If you want your nominee to score the most points, vote only your nominee first and don't list competitors in two through five.

Although all members vote for the winners, there is also a large block of publicists and public relations executives with voting rights. Since the Oscars and publicity are necessary functions of each other, conscience may not always be their guide. Following the release of a promising film, many public relations firms are on studio payrolls for an entire year for the express purpose of running subtle Oscar campaigns.

Another facet of the Academy Awards mostly overlooked by film fans—but not the industry—is increased recognition that an Oscar has lost a decided edge of the prestige it once held. The movie-going public is becoming more discerning as the advent of VCRs and the availability of films on tape allow a wider availability of major films.

For many years, the statuettes (which cost about $60 each) have gone to performers who have been "good citizens" (such as producer/director/writer Oliver Stone) of the oligarchy or to those who have come close to earning an award for a previous performance. They have also been awarded to those who have supported

Hollywood's ultra-liberal political causes — financially and otherwise.

Elizabeth Taylor was awarded an Oscar for *Butterfield 8* in 1960 because of the intense sympathy her throat surgery aroused several months before the awards and for her previous performances in *Raintree County* and *Cat On A Hot Tin Roof.*

Vanessa Redgrave missed several chances at an Oscar because of her outspoken tirades against American involvement in Vietnam, Grenada, Panama and the Arabian Gulf. Although many Hollywood liberals also opposed these involvements, the feeling in the industry was that it was not a British actress's place to damn American foreign policy.

It is a big question why Richard Burton — who seldom gave a bad performance except late in his career — received seven Best Actor nominations, but never a statuette. Many have suggested he was not far enough to the left to satisfy Hollywood liberals.

Many who worked under the old studio system, but are now retired and still maintain their membership, have asked us over the years whether it is possible to "fudge" the process.

We, in turn, asked several people in power.

"When you're into that many people for favors, and that many people are into you for favors, why not?" said a 20th Century-Fox executive, with an off-handed manner that implied there was nothing wrong with cheating.

"You might not be able to guarantee an award, but,

if Mike Ovitz [president of CAA and, at the moment, the most powerful man in Hollywood] and his lieutenants were to let it be known through their network of clients and associates that 'the agency would be pleased' if Whoopi Goldberg received a nomination, that is an 'offer' that can't be refused."

Everyone will undoubtedly have a need for CAA at sometime during their industry career: perhaps a star, a writer, a director or another talent or representation.

Needless to say, Goldberg, a CAA client, was nominated and won the Oscar for Best Supporting Actress in *Ghosts* at the 1991 ceremony. CAA clients won many awards in 1991.

Identical sentiments were echoed at Columbia and Warner Bros. Each of the studio executives were mildly chagrined at the suggestion, but then remarked that — when it came to the possibility of 'fudging the vote' — it would not surprise them and, as one explained, it "is entirely possible and probable."

Academy demographics are getting younger. Many of its recent members (a 30% increase since 1980) are the most successful in the business and are more reliant on Ovitz and CAA for their financing and distribution than on any other single studio. CAA will undoubtedly continue to package deals for those it favors.

Another overlooked aspect which made the Oscar awards suspect was, for several years, that of the nominations for lesser award categories, particularly in the case of documentaries.

The most talked about documentary a few years ago was *Roger & Me,* dealing with an attempt to get the Chairman of General Motors, Roger Smith, on camera following the documentation of hardships caused by the closure of a General Motors plant.

The film was completely ignored by the nominating committee, even though it had received raves from 90% of those who viewed it, including critics. The turn down was largely due to the persuasiveness of Mitchell Block, a member of the screening committee. Block had a glaring conflict of interest.

Block's company, Direct Cinema, owned the United States distribution rights to three of the five nominees for that year in the long film category, but *not* to *Roger & Me.* In digging further, it was discovered that Block had distribution arrangements involving 11 Oscar nominees in the short film documentary category and 13 in the feature documentary category.

Whether the same partiality persisted in other nominee categories we may never know. We can only assume the same prejudice existed — and still exists — in other categories.

How valid is the manner in which the Academy membership is chosen? Are members invited, as intended, to join based on an impartial evaluation of their contributions to the industry?

When Louis B. Mayer first suggested the idea for the Academy to his fellow moguls in 1927, membership was fairly well restricted, but expanded considerably in the 1940s when the awards were first broadcast on radio and the studios began to realize their exploitation value. With the backing of a major studio, literally any office boy could join — and vote their meal ticket. Since the 1950s, membership has been tightened — a little.

In 1979, there were 3,150 members, 30 percent less than 1991's 4,492. One long time, naive — and possibly brain-washed — member explained that "usually, candidates for memberships are sponsored by members of the same branch or craft. The Academy is very important to us and we're cognizant of its vulnerability. To protect it, we must restrict membership to the most talented and outstanding people in the business.

"Possibly," he added, "some joined twenty years ago due to studio pressure to do so, but those cases were rare, and non-existent today."

However, over the years, many young filmmakers have complained that the members are drawn from the almost completely unionized crafts and Guild forces that are totally prejudiced against the mostly non-union independents. They also claim that refusal to enlist them in the unions (largely because they do not have a relative belonging already to sponsor them) forces them to produce their films independently. Their claims are not entirely "sour grapes." By excluding them from the Academy, they are effectively, in practically all cases, shut out from the nominating and winning categories — unless a film is so successful it is impossible to ignore.

Many members of the industry, especially the technicians, consider a nomination to be more important, or a greater honor, than the Oscar itself, since a nomination is made by the members of the individual craft or Guild — except for Best Picture which everyone nominates. It is, therefore, praise from fellow craftsmen — an acknowledgment of respect from working peers. That's their fantasy. Let it lie!

In the selection of eventual winners, *all* branches vote. Since actors make up the largest voting branch, cameramen are not the only technicians who question *everyone's* ability to select best cinematography, etc.

But the most common criticism of the nominations is the charge of "pressure voting" by major studios, public relation firms and talent agencies. Since an Academy Award can mean big financial gain at the box office, increased cassette sales and cable and pay television sales, it is little wonder that many vote the company way under threat of employment cutbacks.

Manipulation? Certainly. Cheating? Obviously.

Studio spokespersons and Academy members have always denied that "pressure voting" existed or exists today. It does. As international editor of a major trade paper several years ago — and a trusted member of the oligarchy — we were privy to several discussions where such machinations were discussed and outlined — but not for publication. 1968 had one glaring example. In that year, seven nominations were given to *Star,* a rather undistinguished, high-budget musical. A filmography of Broadway immortal Gertrude Lawrence, it starred Julie Andrews and a rather mediocre supporting cast. The film was suffering at the box office when 20th Century-Fox put out the word: "Nominate the film in every possible category." Insecure employees did just that.

Critics of the nominating process have often charged that not all eligible voting members cast ballots in the nomination process. The Academy, despite many requests, has always refused to release the figures, claiming that they are known only to the accounting firm of Price Waterhouse & Co.

Those who have requested the figures claim there would be a big disparity between the number of votes for nomination and the number in the final balloting. Many producers and directors claim that those who vote in the nomination process seldom see more than a fraction of the eligible films each year and base their judgement, generally, only on films with which they personally have an association.

When Louis B. Mayer initiated the concept of the Academy, he undoubtedly anticipated the great publicity value of the evolving Academy Awards. It is doubtful, however, that even Mayer anticipated the huge sums which Oscar could and does project for some films.

One executive told us, "Although it is true an Academy Award can add extensive additional revenues to a film, what is important is the quality of the award. The only Oscars that matter are Best Picture, Best Actor and Best Actress."

The point is certainly open for debate. If this is the case, why do theatre marquees emblazen "7 Academy Awards," or whatever, and stress the nominations and awards in newspaper and television advertising in huge type alongside a replica of the Oscar?

Mayer founded the Academy of Motion Picture Arts & Sciences (AMPAS), and its annual awards, because he wanted an organization that would establish him as *the* singular Hollywood power. To that purpose, we believe, he was certainly successful. Mayer's second purpose was to establish a seat of power from which he could combat the rising influence of the guilds and unions which were beginning to inflate studio costs and which the eastern mobs were beginning to infiltrate. In this, he was not so successful.

Politics also plays an important part in Academy decisions. Contemporary social problems have constantly been honored as much for their content in films as for their craftsmanship. *Gandhi, Platoon, In the Heat of the Night, The Deer Hunter, Chariots of Fire* and, earlier, *On the Waterfront* are prime examples. Hollywood liberal politics played a major part in Warren Beatty's Best Director Oscar for *Reds,* based on the life of the United States Communist and expatriate, John Reed.

Most filmgoers do not realize that the Academy membership has consistently ignored many of the world's greatest directors, including Robert Flaherty, Howard Hawks, Fritz Lang, Ernst Lubitsch, Jean Renoir, Orson Welles and Joseph von Sternberg. Alfred Hitchcock, regarded as one of the cinema's greatest directors, was also disregarded, but, finally, awarded a special award. Hitchcock's pictures never carried a message that Hollywood liberals wanted to see on the screen.

Why were these great directors ignored by the Academy, but constantly lauded in histories of the industry? Did none of them exploit themselves with several $4,000 four-color advertisements in *The Hollywood Reporter* and *Variety*? Didn't their films carry the correct liberal message? Or didn't they dine at the correct restaurants and support the proper causes?

Oscar is not only a magnet for money, but also represents the artistic conscience and prestige backbone of a corporate industry. It is an unfortunate marvel that voting members can emasculate and expunge with impunity, perpetuating sham and mediocrity in the world's most intriguing business. Charles Champlin of the *Los Angeles Times* is one that has not allowed the hidden marvel to go unnoticed, properly denouncing the self-interest and spread-eagleism that "masquerade as awards of merit."

The cocktail circuit is also not without its private pith. In 1968, from his base of operations at the Hillcrest Country Club, Groucho Marx excoriated the sorry business as "collective idiocy. There seems to be more fear in this town [for not being nominated or winning] than there was in Germany under Hitler."

In an interview following his Oscar win for *The Godfather,* Marlon Brando added, "You'd think you were going to be sent to Devil's Island and both ears chopped off if you didn't win!"

Recurrent drives by major studios to gain Oscar nominations for films they know are not of Academy caliber are more venal than the costly advertising and word-of-mouth campaigns of the many films which deserve nominations or statuettes. Most studios achieve their goal year after year.

Every time the issue comes up at Oscar time, the Academy's obsequious public relations firm issues sanctimonious denials. In 1980, Academy president Fay Kanin told Steve Edwards on CBS: "I seriously doubt that advertising campaigns have any effect on the nominations. At least, I hope not!"

Rock hard evidence over the years makes such a denial seem ridiculous. But Academy employees and officers who, after all, owe their jobs and allegiances to the studios who finance AMPAS with a levy each year, are not going to admit anything anyway. Therefore, once again, Hollywood has secured itself inside a vacuum. Hard evidence of manipulation of the nominations and final vote seems nonexistent.

However, the record of 20th Century-Fox over the past twenty five years is all the proof required. Now privately held by media mogul Rupert Murdoch, the studio succeeded for over a quarter of a century in foisting terrible — but expensive — films in the "Golden Five" nominations for Best Picture. Each time, it forced out excellent films, at least several of which were Oscar caliber.

In 1964, Fox's *Cleopatra* was nominated for Best Picture by manipulative campaigns among studio employees. *Hud* fell by the wayside. Three years later, *The Sand Pebbles,* an interminably long saga of

American forces in China in 1926, sacrificed the excellent British-Italian *Blowup*. *The Sand Pebbles* had cost Fox so much to produce that the studio was forced to manipulate the nomination in an attempt to recoup some of the cost.

Another Fox turkey of 1969, *Hello, Dolly,* was somehow squeezed in the Best Picture category, probably because Fox was very active in the late sixties and employed a lot of potential voters. The over priced Barbra Streisand turkey shut out Peter Fonda's *Easy Rider* and *They Shoot Horse, Don't They?* (although the late Gig Young won Best Supporting Actor). The excellent British film, *The Prime of Miss Jean Brodie,* should definitely have been nominated for Best Picture and probably would have won. In a lighter vein, the groundbreaking *Bob & Carol & Ted & Alice* should have been a nominee, not to mention *Goodbye Columbus* and *The Sterile Cuckoo.*

But perhaps the most vehement campaign waged for any 20th Century-Fox film was for the studio's *Doctor Dolittle* in 1967. A $16 million bomb, it starred Rex Harrison.

The campaign, however, backfired. John Gregory Dunne was to be allowed to be the "fly on the wall" during the filming of the picture in order to "glorify" 20th Century-Fox in a book—which he had presold— about how a studio operates. The writer followed the film from the first day of shooting to its last bought nomination for an Oscar and put it all together in *The Studio,* which is now a text book and required reading in several film schools around the country.

The Studio revealed, absolutely and devastatingly truthfully, the crass dishonesty of Fox and its publicity department with regard to what they knew to be a bad picture. To this day, Hollywood executives cringe when the subject is broached to them. One public relations man, who was fired by Fox as a scapegoat when the book came out, describes his career as "Before Dunne" and "After Dunne," as do several other public relations executives still working in the industry.

20th Century-Fox traded on studio (and employee) politics, waging shameless advertising campaigns and wooing Oscar nominations (and voters) with expensive food and very private screenings.

Dunne did not have to ask too many questions when he uncovered the experienced hand of Rogers & Cowan in the campaign. This is the same public relations agency that single handedly secured an Oscar nomination and statuette for the first *Rocky* film.

The first sign was a well-positioned and inconsequential announcement in *The Hollywood Reporter* that another Rogers & Cowan client, Bobby Darin, was going to introduce the songs from *Doctor Dolittle* at Princess Grace of Monaco's favorite charity gala for the Red Cross of Monaco. Kelly had also been a client of Rogers & Cowan during her days in film.

In *The Studio,* Dunne described how Fox had waged its *Dolittle* campaign voter by voter — as if it were fighting block by block in a besieged city. In addition, they mailed out copies of the film's soundtrack, ran a massive ad campaign and conducted a telephone campaign voter by voter.

Worst of all, the studio used its influence in the Academy's branches to remove its own *Two For The Road* from preliminary cinematography and editing lists, even though work achieved in those areas far excelled that of work on *Doctor Dolittle*.

The New York critics, upon viewing *Doctor Dolittle,* wrote their reviews in blood. *Time* magazine wrote: "Size and a big budget are no substitutes for originality and charm." The reviews did not discourage Fox from buying a nomination.

Dunne also drew a great deal of information from memos he had been given issued by Jack Hirschberg, a studio publicist, one of which stated: "The following has been decided regarding our Academy Award campaign for *Dolittle.* Each screening for members of the press and Academy branches will be preceded by champagne or cocktails and a midnight buffet supper in the studio commissary. The film is the studio's prime target for an Academy Award consideration."

The studio's battle plan for an Oscar nomination, reported Dunne, was highly successful. He added that, despite very mediocre reviews and lukewarm box office returns, the picture garnered nine nominations — all through manipulation and an outlandish campaign among most members of the various crafts and guilds then working on the lot — certainly not for merit.

The nomination for *Doctor Dolittle* was a big loss for Hollywood, the movie going public and the Academy. To get the film nominated, the members had to overlook *In Cold Blood, Cool Hand Luke, Two For*

The Road and *Thoroughly Modern Millie,* among other fine films of that year.

Stars also enter into the Oscar Derby. In 1984, Warner Bros. took out more ads for Clint Eastwood as Best Actor (seven in *Variety* alone) than any other performer received — and still came up empty handed. Eastwood was bested by Albert Finney for *Under The Volcano.* Warner Bros. was in transition at the time and was not an employer for many of the Academy voting membership.

Again, in 1990, the studio once again launched a campaign to get Eastwood a nomination for *White Hunter, Black Heart,* in which the actor play a fictionalized John Huston directing *The African Queen.* Eastwood's contract with the studio demands that a major advertising campaign be mounted for any picture in which he appears. Extending that provision into the province of the Academy Awards seems natural to a studio publicist.

Another case of manipulation and cheating in its rankest form occurred in 1977, when *Saturday Night Fever* burst upon the screens of the United States and made so much money that even the Academy could not overlook it.

Ordinarily, the Academy, with its voting record, can overlook anything, except a hit — with just a few exceptions.

Saturday Night Fever gave the United States a new type of hero: the daytime loser who becomes a prince of sorts at night. It also introduced a new star: John Travolta. Academy voters tossed the film a bone: a Best Actor nomination for Travolta with the full knowledge he would never receive an Oscar.

But the Academy's music branch was a closed corporation — so to speak — of veterans in the business led by Henry Mancini. They excluded the film totally from competition in any of its categories. Counted out even before the quarter finals, a spokesman for the group — and we hope with tongue in cheek — stated, "They could have played any music during those scenes. We have to consider the appropriateness of the music to the plot."

Anyone who saw the film realized the music *was,* basically, the plot — unless they were deaf, dumb and blind. A more stupid, ignorant or biased remark has never been made by a member of the Academy.

The Gibb Brothers, better known around the world as The Bee Gees, had created an entirely new score for the disco movie, a score that fit the action in every frame of the film. Anyone who has watched Travolta walking through the opening strains of "Stayin' Alive" can never doubt the power of the song or the score as a whole. To exclude the Australian Bee Gees from the category of Best Original Score, the Academy had to nominate a turkey, *Mohammed — Messenger of God,* an obscure, but grandiose, film shot in the Sahara desert.

The nominees for the Best Song were also laughable: The Waltz from *The Slipper and the Rose,* "Someone's Waiting For You," "Candle on the Water," "Nobody Does It Better" and "You Light Up My Life," the eventual winner from a stupid film of the same name which starred unknowns Didi Conn and Joe Silver.

In 1973, the Academy managed to ban Ingmar Bergman's *Scenes From a Marriage* from the voting as an eligible film on a technicality because of the probability that it would win at least four major awards. Critics on both coasts — as well as most industryites — were highly impressed by the three hour film. A random consensus at the time would have assured it awards in the Best Director, Best Picture, Best Actress and Best Film Editing categories.

But many Academy members — and the press — were surprised when they learned that the film had been totally eliminated from the preliminary list of 350 films. A furor erupted. Directors, including Frank Capra and George Cukor, ran advertisements in the trade papers begging the Academy to reconsider. But Academy president Gregory Peck, an old school Hollywood liberal, explained — lamely — that a highly technical point had excluded *Scenes From a Marriage* for consideration.

The film had first been shown as a six part television movie in Sweden earlier (in 1972–73). The date of the film excluded it rather than its origin as a television film. The Academy's board of directors, obviously under pressure from Universal, whose *Sting* was a major contender, would not back down.

Finally, Charles Champlin, Arts Editor of *The Los Angeles Times,* wrote: "As it stands, the luster of the top awards in many categories will be tarnished because Bergman's brilliantly observed and superbly executed drama was not on the ballot. It is crazy and unfair to the winners and losers alike and a seemingly needless blow to the credibility and prestige of the Academy Awards.

"The winners of the 1973 awards, in our opinion, won by default. They were not allowed to compete in merit with the Bergman film. The winner was *The Sting,* from the all-powerful, heavily staffed Universal Pictures."

Actions such as these will go on as long as the Academy of Motion Picture Arts & Sciences and an Academy Award for Merit exist. Cheating and manipulation will exist side by side for the same period of time. Some of it could be excused if the television special at least had merit. But the self-aggrandizement that goes with the acceptance speeches, plus the irrelevant production numbers, produces nothing but boredom. The consistently high ratings around the world remain a constant amazement.

In any case, readers, fans and viewers should bear in mind that the Oscars are also awarded for greed, self-aggrandizement and financial gain by the major studios. They are not all awarded for "merit," as Louis B. Mayer originally intended.

CHAPTER SIX

The Murders on North Elm Drive

> *"For once my father would have to
> congratulate me . . . I carried out
> the perfect murder."*
> — **Judalon Smyth**
>   Quoting Lyle Menendez

Just who was Jose Menendez?

The Hollywood community and Beverly Hills Police Department pressed that issue when Menendez—a relatively little known entertainment executive—was shotgunned to death with his wife, Mary Louise, in their Beverly Hills mansion. From the mutilated condition of the corpses, the murders appeared to be executions.

The bodies of Menendez, 45, and his wife, nicknamed Kitty, 44, were discovered in their North Elm Drive home on August 21, 1989 by their two sons. According to spokesman Lieutenant Robert Curtis, Beverly Hills police received "a hysterical call" on 911 and arrived on the scene about one minute later to discover the bodies in the family room of their Mediterranean-style mansion. Although the house was worth several million dollars, it appeared to be furnished by the high-powered Cuban and his wife in early Salvation Army and Goodwill castoffs.

Both Menendez and his wife had been shot repeatedly "throughout the body," said Craig Harvey, acting investigative supervisor for the Los Angeles County Coroner's Office. Later statements and autopsy reports revealed that the face and brain of Jose Menendez had been practically blown away by a shotgun blast in the mouth. It was also rumored that he had been shot in the genitals with a 12-gauge shotgun. A friend of a Beverly Hills policeman was also told that Kitty had received a blast in the vagina and that her face, too, had been blown away.

The Beverly Hills Police Department was aware of one unusual circumstance at the scene of the crime: all the shell casings had been removed. The police had never known this to happen before in an execution slaying. It was a major question mark to the police during the early stages of the investigation. Except for this single, out-of-character fact, it might have been a professional "execution." Professional "hit men," however, have seldom been known to remove shell casings.

The murder scene was a horrendous sight for investigators. Menendez was slumped at one end of an L-shaped sectional couch in the family television room. Kitty Menendez's body was found on the floor a few feet from the sofa. She appeared to have risen from the couch headed for a pantry a few yards away. There was no indication of a struggle, nor evidence of a burglary. Both bodies were casually dressed in street clothes.

Menendez, an avid tennis player, was wearing tennis shorts.

The Coroner's office estimated the time of death to be somewhere between eight and eleven p.m. Both victims were declared dead at the scene at 11:50 p.m.— three minutes after officers arrived.

The Menendez sons were taken to police headquarters a few blocks away and questioned, but were not considered suspects in the murder. Lyle, 21, and Erik, 18, were released an hour or so later. They stood, collectively, to inherit an estate worth approximately $14 million. Fratricide and matricide for financial gain was not an unknown motive for murder, so they were not forgotten by the investigators.

In their search for a motive, detectives called the Los Angeles Police Department's Organized Crime Intelligence Division to determine whether or not the Division had any information on Menendez; the reply was negative.

At the time of his death, Jose Menendez was Chairman of LIVE Entertainment, Inc. of Van Nuys, California, a rapidly expanding firm of 2,000 employees which purchased video rights to feature films and delivered video and music tapes to retailers.

LIVE Entertainment was 49% owned by Carolco, founded in the late 1970s by Mario Kassar and Andrew Vajna. The pair had arrived in Hollywood from unknown parts of the globe around 1975. Carolco was originally formed to sell foreign rights to motion pictures at such venues as The Cannes Film Festival and MIFED, the international trade fair for films and television held annually in Milan, Italy.

Carolco produced, among other films, the financially successful *Rambo* series, which starred Sylvester Stallone. It also produced the two *Terminator* films starring Arnold Schwarzenegger. The two partners were successful and had made millions of dollars since they arrived in Hollywood.

A few days following the slayings, the police were no further along in their investigation, but a spokesman insisted that the couple were slain "in a fashion typical of mob style executions." The police, nevertheless, kept an eye focused on the Menendez brothers, Erik and Lyle.

Homicide detectives deduced that it had been two killers, wielding 12-gauge shot guns, who confronted the victims, or crept up on them as they watched television.

The official silence in such a high profile case led to widespread belief that the Menendezes were executed in a slaying that was somehow related to the executive's past or present business activities. Or else they had a suspect or suspects in mind, but were not yet ready to tip their hands. The break in the case, however, was to come from an unusual and surprising source.

Carolco executives Kassar and Vajna adamantly refused to discuss any aspect of the slayings with reporters. Carolco president Peter Hoffman stated, "We don't care to say any more [about it] except it's a dangerous, vicious world we live in, and we're all subject to bizarre events."

Whether or not Hoffman was intimating that there had been threats against Menendez or other members of the company was not disclosed — either by himself or the Beverly Hills Police Department.

The homicides certainly not only bared Menendez's fast-track performance since he had become involved with Carolco, but also revealed his record as a top executive in RCA's Record Division. His death made public many practices of RCA (and the music industry in general) including bloated record sales figures. Menendez had left RCA under a cloud as questions had been raised about his accounting methods.

Menendez was edged out as executive vice president and "de facto" chief operation officer of the company shortly after General Electric purchased RCA in 1986. Elliot Goldman, who became president and CEO five days before the purchase, said a clash of styles between he and Menendez was largely responsible for the departure of Menendez from the company.

"He was very intelligent and had a lot of energy. But he really kept a very tight rein on everything. His style was not appropriate for the kind of company I wanted to build up," explained Goldman. He also confirmed reports by other RCA executives that Menendez was discovered to have engaged in a common record industry tactic: shipping too many units — a ploy which makes immediate sales look good, even though later heavy returns will deflate the numbers. In Menendez's case, a $25 million "write down" resulted in the first six months after he left the company, displeasing many recording artists who had relied on royalties from those returned records.

But Hoffman found charges of "questionable practices" at RCA "laughable." He attributed the claims to personality clashes and management style among RCA executives.

The year following the disagreement with Goldman, Menendez quit at the expiration of his contract and was hired by Carolco to head the turn around of International Video Entertainment (IVE). When Menendez took over, IVE was a failing video company that Vajna and Kassar had purchased in 1986 from Noel C. Bloom. Bloom, a businessman from the San Fernando Valley, had started his video empire as "a purveyor of sexually explicit cassettes." From the enormous profits, he had gradually branched out into other lines.

A securities analyst said IVE was "a mess" when Menendez took it over. Carolco, according to the analyst, acquired the company while its earnings were "dipping" in the hope and belief it could turn the company around. Menendez immediately created a lot of ill will by slashing the company payroll from 550 to 167. He also eliminated expensive offices in the Woodland Hills area.

At the same time, Menendez was using Carolco's strong connections with "mainstream" Hollywood to

Mary Astor during her custody battle with Dr. Franklyn Thorpe. (Marvin Paige's Motion Picture & TV Research Service)

Marilyn and Mary Astor on the child's fourth birthday. (Marvin Paige's Motion Picture & TV Research Service)

Dr. Franklyn Thorpe (l.) and Mary Astor (r.) with their daughter Marilyn. Superior Judge Goodwin J. ("Goody") Knight (c.) was later elected Governor of California. (Marvin Paige's Motion Picture & TV Research Service)

Left: Ruth Chatterton and Walter Huston in *Dodsworth.* Huston and Mary Astor were lovers during the filming and while her custody battle was in process. (Marvin Paige's Motion Picture & TV Research Service) *Left, top:* Darryl F. Zanuck. (Marvin Paige's Motion Picture & TV Research Service) *Top Right:* Jean Harlow and Paul Bern. (John Austin Collection)

Clara Bow and Rex Bell following their wedding. Author Elinor Glynn claimed that Bell had more "It" than Clara. (Marvin Paige's Motion Picture & TV Research Service)

Clara Bow, the "It Girl." "We did as we damn well pleased," she said of Hollywood in the 1930s. (Marvin Paige's Motion Picture & TV Research Service)

Roscoe "Fatty" Arbuckle, who was manipulated by Paramount chief Adolph Zukor in order to negate his $3 million contract. (Marvin Paige's Motion Picture & TV Research Service)

Cliff Robertson, who was literally banished from the film industry for five years. (Marvin Paige's Motion Picture & TV Research Service)

Jack L. Warner, along with his brothers Harry and Sam, founded Warner Bros. Pictures, Inc. (Marvin Paige's Motion Picture & TV Research Service)

The disliked Harry Cohn (l.) with Joe E. Brown. Mafioso Johnny Roselli came to Cohn's rescue to buy out one of his Columbia Pictures partners. The $500,000 arrived in a suitcase sent by mobster Abner "Longie" Zwillman. (Marvin Paige's Motion Picture & TV Research Service)

Cecil B. DeMille, who made the first film shot in Hollywood, *The Squaw Man,* shown directing Yul Brynner in the fine art of sword play. (Marvin Paige's Motion Picture & TV Research Service)

Top right: Rock Hudson. Universal Pictures managed to keep Rock Hudson's homosexuality a secret for thirty years. (John Austin Collection) *Top left:* MGM production chief Irving Thalberg (l.) and his wife, actress Norma Shearer, with Louis B. Mayer (r.). Mayer was the driving force behind the formation of the Academy of Motion Picture Arts and Sciences. *Left:* Albert Dekker in 1967, a year before his death. (both: Marvin Paige's Motion Picture & TV Research Service)

Albert Dekker (r.) in one of his early pictures *Campus Mystery.* Scott Colton (l.) and Mary Russell co-starred in the Columbia film. (John Austin Collection)

Will Hays (l.), the morals czar of the film industry, his wife and Jack L. Warner (r.). (Marvin Paige's Motion Picture & TV Research Service)

Raquel Welch in *Kansas City Bomber*. (John Austin Collection)

Mae West with neophyte British director of *Myra Breckinridge*, Michael Sarne. Sarne was totally inept and created constant confusion. (John Austin Collection)

Top right: Raquel, following her marriage in Paris to Patrick Curtis. (John Austin Collection) *Top left:* During the filming of *Myra Breckinridge.* (John Austin Collection) *Left:* Debra Winger in *Cannery Row,* the catalyst for Welch's law suit against the Metro-Goldwyn-Mayer Film Co. Winger replaced Welch in the role of Suzy. (Marvin Paige's Motion Picture & TV Research Service)

Left: "What! Me? Sue?" *Bottom left:* Mae West in *Myra Breckinridge.* West and Welch feuded constantly over wardrobe problems. *Below (l. to r.):* At the post filming party for *Myra Breckinridge:* Raquel Welch, studio chief Richard Zanuck, Mae West and producer Richard Fryer. (photos: John Austin Collection)

Sarah Miles in *The Man Who Loved Cat Dancing.* Arizona officials have since stated that MGM master-minded a major cover-up over the cause of her manager's death. (John Austin Collection)

Mae West in 1948 aboard the Queen Mary. (John Austin Collection)

Shary Marshall, who co-starred with Steve Cochran in *Tell Me In The Sunlight*. The film was never released theatrically, but can be found in some video stores. (John Austin Collection)

Sarah Miles and Burt Reynolds in *The Man Who Loved Cat Dancing*. (Marvin Paige's Motion Picture & TV Research Service)

Cochran (r.) in one of his most popular films, *The Damned Don't Cry,* in which he was featured with stars Joan Crawford and David Brian. (Marvin Paige's Motion Picture & TV Research Service)

Cochran in *Slander* for MGM. (John Austin Collection)

In *Slander,* Cochran co-starred with Van Johnson and Ann Blyth. (John Austin Collection)

The author (l.) with Mae West and Regis Philbin during her last film, *Sextette.* (John Austin Collection)

Vanessa Redgrave in *Camelot*. Redgrave has consistently snuffed her chances for an Oscar by badmouthing Zionism, condemning Israel, and questioning government policies in Grenada, Panama and Iraq. (Marvin Paige's Motion Picture & TV Research Service)

Jon Voight in *Runaway Train*. Cannon Films spent thousands in an attempt to get Voight an Oscar as Best Actor. (John Austin Collection)

Gregory Peck, one of Hollywood's consistent liberals, received an Oscar for *To Kill A Mockingbird*. (Marvin Paige's Motion Picture & TV Research Service.)

Panoramic shot from 20th Century-Fox's *The Sand Pebbles* with Richard Crenna in the foreground. The film was maneuvered into a Best Picture nomination. (Marvin Paige's Motion Picture & TV Research Service)

Elizabeth Taylor in *Butterfield 8,* one of her more mediocre
performances. (Marvin Paige's Motion Picture & TV Research Service)

Rex Harrison in *Doctor Dolittle,* a Fox bomb which the studio managed to get nominated as Best Picture. (Marvin Paige's Motion Picture & TV Research Service)

Joanne Woodward in her Oscar-winning performance from *The Three Faces Of Eve.* She and husband Paul Newman have long been members of Hollywood's liberal majority. (Marvin Paige's Motion Picture & TV Research Service)

Dan Aykroyd received an Oscar nomination for *Driving Miss Daisy* as soon as he signed up with Mike Ovitz and his CAA Agency. (Marvin Paige's Motion Picture & TV Research Service)

The coveted statuette, which costs the Academy of Motion Picture Arts and Sciences about $60. (© AMPAS)

20th Century-Fox's *Cleopatra,* which was nominated as a result of a highly manipulative campaign. (Marvin Paige's Motion Picture & TV Research Service)

Hollywood's new "Golden Boy" Kevin Costner in *Dances With Wolves.* (John Austin Collection)

Julie Andrews in *Star*, another Fox film which used manipulation to get a nomination. (Marvin Paige's Motion Picture & TV Research Service)

John Travolta and Karen Gorney in a scene from *Saturday Night Fever*. The leaders of the Academy Music Branch refused to nominate the film in the music category. (Marvin Paige's Motion Picture & TV Research Service)

Henry Mancini, leader of the "Old Boy" Network Academy Music Branch. (John Austin Collection)

The author (l.) on location in New Mexico with Clint Eastwood. Eastwood's contracts with studios demand a major Oscar advertising campaign for each picture. (John Austin Collection)

The five nominees for the 1963 Oscar for Best Actor: Peter O'Toole, Burt Lancaster, Gregory Peck, Jack Lemmon and Marcello Mastroianni. Many thought Peter O'Toole deserved it for *Lawrence of Arabia.* "Politically correct" Gregory Peck got the nod for *To Kill A Mockingbird.* (Marvin Paige's Motion Picture & TV Research Service)

Lyle Menendez and his father, José. (John Austin Collection)

Erik and Lyle Menendez. (John Austin Collection)

The Menendez mansion on Elm Drive in Beverly Hills. (John Austin Collection)

Tracy Scoggins. She was sent home from a guest stint on *Magnum, P.I.* when she wouldn't "cooperate" sexually. (Marvin Paige's Motion Picture & TV Research Service)

Top left: Vince Edwards. Andrew Prine importuned Karen to allow a process server access to Edwards, who was dating Prine's estranged wife. *Bottom left:* Actor Mark Goddard, who, with his wife, discovered Karyn's body. (both: Marvin Paige's Motion Picture & TV Research Service) *Top right:* Andrew Prine, Karyn's last boy friend, as he appeared in *The Wide Country* television series. (John Austin Collection)

Karyn Kupcinet (l.) with Jerry Lewis and two unidentified cast members on *The Ladies Man* set. (John Austin Collection)

Jerry Lewis, a friend of the Kupcinet family. (John Austin Collection)

Theresa Saldana in *The Evil That Men Do.* She was almost killed by a Scottish drifter who continues to threaten her from prison. (Marvin Paige's Motion Picture & TV Research Service)

Oscar winner Jodie Foster. A president was almost assassinated because of a crazed fan's "erotomania" over the actress. (John Austin Collection)

Actress Rebecca Schaeffer was gunned down by a crazed "fanterrorist." (Marvin Paige's Motion Picture & TV Research Service)

Sylvester Stallone has spent thousands on security precautions because of terrorist threats. (Marvin Paige's Motion Picture & TV Research Service)

Thom Bierdz, of *The Young And The Restless,* shown with Lauralee Bell. His brother bludgeoned their mother to death and told Thom that he was next. (John Austin Collection)

Richard Gere & Julia Roberts in *Pretty Woman,* which had no violence and was one of the highest grossing pictures of 1990. (John Austin Collection)

Catherine Deneuve. A crazed "fanterrorist" threw a rock through the windshield of her car. (Marvin Paige's Motion Picture & TV Research Service)

Mary Hart, of *Entertainment Tonight,* has also been threatened by "fanterrorists." (John Austin Collection)

Candice Bergen was followed by a "fanterrorist," but foiled him by keeping a cool head. (Marvin Paige's Motion Picture & TV Research Service)

Jayne Mansfield.

Jayne and Tommy Noonan in *Promises! Promises!*, a jinxed film.
(Marvin Paige's Motion Picture & TV Research Service)

Jayne Mansfield, with Tony Randall, in one of her first major films, *Will Success Spoil Rock Hunter?*, in which she reprised her Broadway role.
(Marvin Paige's Motion Picture & TV Research Service)

Loni Anderson, who recreated Mansfield's life for television. (Marvin Paige's Motion Picture & TV Research Service)

Loni Anderson and Arnold Schwarzenegger (as Mickey Hargitay) in *The Jayne Mansfield Story,* a television movie. (Marvin Paige's Motion Picture & TV Research Service)

Tony Randall and Jayne in *Will Success Spoil Rock Hunter?* (Marvin Paige's Motion Picture & TV Research Service)

Jayne and Mickey are greeted by her daughter, Jayne Marie, on their return from a USO tour of the Far East. (John Austin Collection)

Jayne, in a Marineland publicity shot. (John Austin Collection)

Sophia Loren admires Jayne's attributes at a Hollywood function.
(John Austin Collection)

Left: Mamie Van Doren, for whom Jayne substituted on the ill-fated southern night club appearances. (Marvin Paige's Motion Picture & TV Research Service) *Bottom:* Jayne and Mickey Hargitay during a happy part of their marriage. (John Austin Collection)

Left: Chuck Norris, one of the few stars big enough to espouse his conservative views and not be blacklisted. (John Austin Collection) *Bottom:* ...As is Tom Selleck (l.), shown with Steve Guttenberg (c.) and Ted Danson (r.). (John Austin Collection)

...As well as Arnold Schwarzenegger (r.), shown with Carl Weathers (l.). (John Austin Collection)

Louis B. Mayer (r.), head of Metro-Goldwyn-Mayer, during a pre-war visit with Winston Churchill. Mayer insisted on Robert Taylor completing *Song of Russia* before he left for the armed forces. (Marvin Paige's Motion Picture & TV Research Service)

Charlton Heston, another star too big to be blacklisted by the liberals. (John Austin Collection)

Robert Taylor and Susan Peters in *Song of Russia,* a film the United States government insisted be finished. (Marvin Paige's Motion Picture & TV Research Service)

Director George Cukor (c.), for whom Lorimar renamed the Robert Taylor Building at MGM. Even though it was fifty years "after the fact," liberals objected to the building's being named after Taylor because of his testimony before the HUAC. Cukor is shown with Candice Bergen (l.) and Jacqueline Bisset.

Actor Howard da Silva, one of the actors named as a communist sympathizer by Robert Taylor. (above and left: Marvin Paige's Motion Picture & TV Research Service)

Oscar-winning director Oliver
Stone, the current favorite of
the liberal Hollywood establishment. (John Austin
Collection)

"Lord, how we honor ourselves!"
Bob Hope (r.) presenting an
honorary Oscar to Charles
"Buddy" Rogers for his philan-
thropy over the years, Rogers
was married to the late Mary
Pickford. (John Austin Collection)

Dmytryk (l.) with Lew Ayres,
on the set of *The Carpetbaggers,*
which he helmed for Para-
mount Pictures. (Marvin
Paige's Motion Picture & TV
Research Service)

Ginger Rogers (r.) and her
mother. Lela Rogers refused to
allow Ginger to say a line of
communist propaganda in
Tender Comrade. (Marvin
Paige's Motion Picture & TV
Research Service)

Edward Dmytryk (l.) directing Dick Powell in *Cornered* for RKO. He exiled himself to the United Kingdom following the House Unamerican Activities Committee hearings. Dmytryk was truly an innocent victim of the era and blacklisting. (Marvin Paige's Motion Picture & TV Research Service)

Pat Boone. "I have been blackballed from movie and TV roles. Liberals don't want me around." (Marvin Paige's Motion Picture & TV Research Service)

sign multiple picture deals with film makers such as producer Ed Pressman (*Wall Street* and *Wired*) and director Taylor Hackford for video rights to their films.

Jose Menendez had arrived in the United States in 1960. At sixteen, he was sleeping in a Pennsylvania farm house attic. Menendez's father, Jose Francisco, a former world class soccer player, and his mother, Maria Carlotta, a former Olympic swimmer, sent Menendez to the United States to prevent him from becoming a communist in Fidel Castro's Cuba. A little more than ten years later, Menendez was the president of his own company.

In an interview following Menendez's murder, his son, Erik, said, "He [Menendez] used to tell us [Erik and his brother, Lyle] that when he came to the United States from Cuba in 1960 he didn't speak much English. But he said he made it his goal to run one of the largest companies in America."

After finishing high school, Menendez was eager to begin work. He was already a winning salesman in high school, selling encyclopedias for spending money. But Jose Menendez was persuaded to enter college and obtain an education which would help him in his ambitions. He majored in accounting.

While in college in Illinois, he met Mary Louise in a philosophy class. A short time later, they were married. Following college graduation, the couple moved to New York, where Kitty worked as a school teacher and Menendez completed studies in 1967 for his degree in accounting at Queens College.

Five years later, Menendez was named president of a small container company. He went on to spend fourteen years with RCA, eventually serving as the head of RCA/Ariola Records until 1986.

Hired by Carolco, Menendez and his family moved from Princeton, New Jersey—against Kitty's wishes—and rented a house in Calabasas, just north of the San Fernando Valley. Calabasas is an upper middle class suburb of Los Angeles, across a small mountain range from Malibu. Jose purchased a thirteen acre tract, on the top of which he built a large house with a spectacular view over a small mountain range to the Pacific Ocean. The house was barely finished when the family abandoned the area and moved to the Elm Drive house.

The Mediterranean-style house with a red Spanish tiled roof contained six bedrooms, a large courtyard, a parking lot suitable for a small shopping mall, a tennis court, a swimming pool and a guesthouse. Built during the Beverly Hills real estate boom of the late 1920s, and rebuilt in 1974, it had previously been rented by Elton John, rock star Prince and director Hal Prince. An Arabian prince also checked in at $35,000 per month, replete with harem, prior to the Menendez purchase. The house had come to be known as "The House of Princes."

Two events forced the family to move to Beverly Hills. Erik and Lyle became involved in two serious criminal offenses which were major felonies: a burglary at the home of Michael Warren Ginsberg in Calabasas and grand theft at the home of John List in Hidden Hills.

Police reports revealed more that $100,000 in money and jewelry taken from the two houses in burglaries committed by the two brothers. Even in that neighborhood of million dollar-plus homes, this was not an insignificant amount. The felonies certainly constituted the kind for which most defendants would have done a stretch in a county prison farm.

Jose dealt was his sons' "transgressions," as he referred to them, the way he would deal with any tough, sticky business problem. "Jose minimized the damage and pressed forward, fixing something that was broken without actually 'dealing with the problem,'" related a former Calabasas acquaintance of the family.

The money and the jewels were returned to their rightful owners and around $11,000 paid in damages to the victims. Since Erik was underage at the time, the family decided that he would "take the fall" for both brothers, allowing Jose to preserve his dream of having Lyle accepted into Princeton University. The college was only a mile or two from the family's former 16-room estate which had been purchased while Jose was riding high with RCA Records. An expensive Beverly Hills criminal attorney, Gerald Chaleff, was hired to represent Erik. Everything "was worked out" exactly as Jose Menendez has orchestrated it. Erik received a short term of probation and compulsory counseling. Kitty asked her psychologist to recommend someone her son could consult for the required number of hours ordered by the court. Dr. Jerome Oziel of Beverly Hills was recommended — a referral that was to have far reaching consequences.

Following the murders, many people in the entertainment industry were questioned about their knowledge of the little known Cuban.

Sylvester Stallone, a large stockholder in Carolco since the success of the *Rambo* projects, was one of those questioned. As a director of Carolco, he was asked if he could shed any light on the case. It was thought the actor might have knowledge of any business deals proposed by Menendez prior to his death. Any such deals would have to be approved by the board. What Stallone revealed, if anything, was never released by Beverly Hills Police Department detectives.

Many of those questioned said Menendez was an extremely aggressive boss and deal maker. Whereas friends saw him as an influential leader, adversaries occasionally saw an over-reacher who cut jobs, cut corners and broke his word on his way to the top.

An executive of Broadcast Music, Inc., who worked with Menendez for several years at RCA Records in New York, said, "If you took a poll, a lot of people whose toes were stepped on by Jose would have to tell you they didn't like him." Peter Hoffman, the president of Carolco, said that Menendez could very often be insensitive and generally reached for every advantage in a transaction. In an interview with the *Los Angeles Times* several days after the killings, however, he added that Menendez "was very self conscious, self confident and charismatic in the way he dealt with things."

"In my judgement," said Hoffman, "these are assets, not liabilities."

Because of his aggressiveness, Menendez turned the corner for IVE Entertainment, by now renamed LIVE. From a loss of $20 million in 1986, the company showed an $8 million profit in 1987, and doubled that in 1988.

The official silence following five days of investigation in such a high profile case led to widespread belief that Menendez was executed in a slaying that could somehow have been related to his past or present business activities.

Jose also had a penchant for mistresses — as was the custom with many wealthy, upper class Cubans. This was a constant source of friction in the Menendez marriage. Facets of an unsavory family life were rampant following the tragedy and painted an ugly picture of Jose Menendez as a family man.

In the weeks following the deaths, the ongoing theory by everyone connected to them (except, perhaps, the Beverly Hills Police Department — and they weren't talking) was that they had been mob hits. No other theory was advanced by anyone.

Except for Erik Menendez.

The younger Menendez son pointed the finger at Noel Bloom, who was a former associate of the ruling Mafia family in Los Angeles, the Bonnano organization. Early in the investigation, Erik told the police, as well as reporters, that Bloom and his father loathed each other following a business deal over an unpaid debt IVE had agreed to pay and over the distribution rights to a children's film which was supposed to have gone to Bloom, but which Menendez would not surrender.

Erik and Lyle moved from location to location fearing, they explained, retaliation by the mob once Erik's remarks were revealed.

At the time of his death, Menendez headed a company that had purchased two firms that had previously been strongly linked with organized crime, adding fuel to the speculative fire of a mob-connected "hit."

Following the first of two memorial services in Los Angeles for Jose and Kitty, Jose's sister said she felt that her brother and his wife were killed because Jose refused to do business with mobsters who had heavily infiltrated the video industry. The sister, Marta Menendez-Cano, of West Palm Beach, Florida, said that, in her opinion, her brother angered many mobsters when he took over IVE (which had previously distributed X-rated films) and then cleaned house. Organized crime reaps millions from X-rated and pornographic videos throughout the country. When Menendez took over IVE for Carolco, he dropped this "sideline" completely. "Because of his success, he probably stepped on many toes, which many people didn't like," Menendez-Cano remarked.

However, before leaving for the second memorial service in Princeton, New Jersey, where the family had lived for years, Lyle Menendez said he did not believe his aunt's theory was *entirely* correct. Still, he remarked, the family was convinced that the slayings were "calculated." "Someone was trying to send a message," he said. But no one in the family has been able to "decipher that message," he added, resignedly.

Much of the speculation concerning a possible mob connection in the Menendez murders was caused by two events: LIVE's purchase of Strawberries, a New England based music and video retail chain and a pending law suit, Noel Bloom vs. Carolco et al.

Strawberries was sold to LIVE Entertainment by Morris Levy for $40.5 million dollars. Levy was convicted in May, 1988, of conspiring to extort more than a million dollars from MCA Records, Inc.* He was also under investigation by a grand jury for connections to organized crime.

"All I know about Levy is what I read in the papers," one of the Menendez sons said. "I don't know if there is any connection to us. That's all I can say. That's all I know."

But Vicki Greenleaf, spokeswoman for LIVE, said the company had hired a law firm that specialized in white collar crime to investigate Strawberries before it made the purchase, after which Levy had nothing to do with the company.

---

* For further indication of mob activity within MCA, Inc., prior to its purchase by Matsushita, see *Dark Victory: Ronald Reagan, MCA and the Mob* by Dan Moldea (Viking, 1986).

"The intimation that the Strawberries deal had anything to do with [it] is absolutely ridiculous," said David Lieberman, LIVE Entertainment executive vice president and consultant. "Levy wanted to sell; we wanted to buy. It was a normal negotiation."

(LIVE Entertainment was formed earlier when IVE, through Menendez, bought Lieberman's Minneapolis-based music and video company and merged it with IVE.)

Levy was sentenced to ten years in federal prison and fined $200,000 for conspiring to extort money from a Philadelphia-area record distributor. According to court records and law enforcement agencies, he acted as a business front for Vincent (The Chin) Gigante, reputed by law enforcement officials to be the underboss of the Genovese crime family.

In another twist, ten days after the murders, LIVE Entertainment announced that it had retained the prestigious New York law firm of Paul, Weiss, Rifkind, Wharton & Garrison to conduct an internal inquiry in the Menendez slaying. The law firm was the same one that represented Morris Levy when he was convicted of extortion charges.

Prior to his death, Menendez had also become deeply entangled in the already existing dispute with Noel Bloom stemming from Carolco's purchase of his video company. In 1987, Bloom sued Carolco, alleging a breach of contract on its part by failing to pay an outstanding loan to a third party. Menendez became involved in the litigation when Bloom charged that he had blocked Bloom from acquiring rights from Hasbro to a children's film called *G.I. Joe, the Movie*. Bloom claimed in his suit that Menendez was trying to hold him to a "non-compete" clause provision of the sales agreement, which is standard in most sales agreements. At the same time, Menendez tried to force Hasbro to give IVE the film for $100,000, despite an earlier verbal agreement by an IVE officer to pay $500,000 for it.

In September, 1988, a court referee found in favor of Bloom, stating in open court that Menendez had engaged in "highly inappropriate" conduct and a "squeeze play" in trying to reduce his own verbal deal. The law suit clearly left strong animosities on both sides.

In his short time in Hollywood, Menendez had not made many friends outside the Carolco circle.

According to a filing with the Securities and Exchange Commission, LIVE had purchased a $15 million key man life insurance policy on Menendez, whose employment contract with LIVE extended to December 31, 1991 at a salary of $500,000 plus generous bonuses for performance.

Beneficiaries of the policy, according to Peter Hoffman, were Bankers Trust Co. of New York and European-based Credit Lyonnais Bank Nederland, both of which were LIVE creditors. There was also supposed to be a second $5 million policy with beneficiaries to be named by Menendez. However, the family was to receive a shock several days after the death.

On that afternoon, Lyle and Erik Menendez, accompanied by two uncles, Kitty's brother Brian Andersen and Jose's brother-in-law Carlos Baralt, who was the executor of Jose's will, met with officials of LIVE at the company's headquarters. They wanted to discuss Jose's financial situation.

At the meeting, the heirs were informed that the second policy of $5 million had never gone into effect. Jose Menendez had not taken the required physical examination. He had mistakenly believed that the physical he had taken for the first policy was good for both. He did not realize that each policy was with a different insurer and required a separate physical.

According to an associate inside the company who attended the meeting, the announcement was greeted with a resounding silence. Erik and Lyle had obviously expected the $5 million policy to be paid on Jose's death. It was a crushing disappointment.

Another twist in the double murder was uncovered several months later. In December, word reached the police that Lyle had made a sudden trip back to Los Angeles from Princeton and "destroyed something" in the family computer.

Lyle had told a friend from Princeton, Glenn Stevens, that a relative (believed to be Brian Andersen) had discovered "a new will and I went there and erased it!"

"I was in disbelief and just laughed," said Stevens in an interview, also relating that Lyle displayed signs of nervousness as he discussed the incident. In a somber moment, Stevens recalled, Lyle said, "My father wasn't very happy with me."

With the payment of a $400,000 insurance policy, Lyle went on a spending spree which included a Porsche Carrera, a Rolex watch, $40,000 in clothes and the purchase of a Princeton cafe. Queried on the purchases, he replied, "It's consistent with the way I've led most of my life. I like quality things. I don't feel it's ostentatious."

Brian Andersen equated Lyle's spending spree, which he put at over $500,000, as the only way Lyle knew of acting out the rage he felt over the loss of his parents. "My speculation is that a little of what we're seeing in Lyle is trying to move too fast, is sort of a way to reach out because he's angry."

Detectives called in a computer expert to attempt to retrieve the document in the computer, but without success. They believe that whatever was in the computer regarding the Menendez will was intentionally destroyed in such a way to be irretrievable.

Following their usual custom, police declined comment directly on any aspect of the case. However, the brutality of the murders—including the *coup de grace* of a shotgun blast into Jose Menendez's mouth, kept everyone believing that they were a "message killing."

On March 8, 1990, all theories were thrown out the window when the Beverly Hills Police Department issued arrest warrants for Erik and Lyle Menendez for the murder of their parents. Lyle had been under surveillance and was taken into custody as he left the Elm Drive home in Erik's Jeep Wrangler with two friends who were not held. He was booked at the West Hollywood Sheriff's sub-station.

An arrest warrant was also issued for Erik, who was competing in a tennis tournament in Israel. Hearing of his brother's arrest, Erik contacted Gerald Chaleff and said he would return to the United States and surrender to police.

Following the arrest, Olson stated, "We're on real solid ground," but refused to elaborate. He revealed, however, that the brothers had been under suspicion since the first day of the investigation.

Beverly Hills Police Chief Marvin Ianone told a packed news conference at Beverly Hills Police Headquarters, "I've been in this business for over thirty years and I have heard of very few murders that were more savage than this one." As for the motive, Ianone said that "if there was a sole motive or several motives" it or they had not been determined.

Ianone noted that it was "no big secret that the Menendezes had an estate that was worth millions of dollars and that the two brothers were the sole beneficiaries. . .There have been all kinds of theories from day one about this case."

The break in the case had come the previous Thursday, when a thirty-seven year old woman, Judalon Rose Smyth (pronounced "Smith") had been going through an entangled love affair and had talked to the police.

Judalon Smyth's alleged lover was Dr. Jerome Oziel—the same Dr. Oziel whom Kitty Menendez's psychologist had recommended to her a year earlier as the doctor for Erik. During the brief counseling sessions, Oziel had met the entire Menendez family.

Judalon Smyth was an unknown to Erik and Lyle. Yet, seven months from the time of the double murder on Elm Drive, she would be responsible for their arrest on murder charges for slaughtering their parents.

Three days before Lyle's arrest, Smyth contacted the Beverly Hills investigators and told them of the existence of audiotapes in the Bedford Drive office of Dr. Oziel. On those tapes, said Smyth, the Menendez brothers had allegedly confessed to the murders of their parents. She also told the police that the brothers had threatened to kill Oziel if he reported them.

None of Smyth's information, apparently, was known to the authorities after seven months of investigation.

A subpoena was obtained to search all of Oziel's premises. The tapes were eventually found in a safe-deposit box in a bank in the San Fernando Valley in Sherman Oaks near Oziel's home. According to his records, about two months after the murders, on Halloween of 1989, Erik telephoned Oziel for an urgent appointment. Judalon Smyth claimed she was in the office at the time of Erik's call, although Oziel would later deny it. Smyth told authorities that Oziel told her that he hoped it wasn't what he feared it was going to be. "That was the first time Jerry indicated that he, too, thought the boys had done it," said Smyth.

On his arrival at the office, Erik did not want to talk inside, and suggested they go for a walk. During the walk, he confessed that he and his brother carried out the murders. On their return to the office, Oziel made Erik call his brother and have him come immediately to the office. It was then that Smyth claims she overheard the confessions by listening in the next office at the request of Oziel. Erik revealed in detail the planning and execution of the crime, including the fabricated alibi defense of attending *Batman* in Century City and then attended a Food Fair at Santa Monica Civic Auditorium.

In the affidavits before the Second District Court of Appeal, Oziel claimed doctor/patient confidentiality. The Court — following a decision by a Los Angeles Superior Court Judge that the tapes were inadmissible because of that time-honored relationship — overruled the decision and said the tapes were admissible into evidence because there was an "implied threat to the doctor of bodily harm" if he revealed their contents. The Court decided that this negated the confidentiality tenet.

Defense attorneys for both Erik and Lyle immediately appealed to the California Supreme Court and that appeal is yet to be acted upon.

On the day following the boys' "confession," Smyth says Oziel warned her in a threatening manner not to tell anyone what she had heard. But Smyth did tell two friends who rented space in her office. They advised her to go to the police.

Judalon Smyth took her information one step further. In a televised interview on ABC-TV's *Prime Time Live,* she claimed she overheard everything the brothers told Oziel following Lyle's arrival at the office.

Smyth again claimed that Oziel, in spite of his denials, had instructed her to sit in a nearby room and eavesdrop on the discussion he had with Lyle and Erik on October 31st. She told *Prime Time Live,* "Erik said that Lyle made him take the first shot. I suppose that's because Lyle thought that if he didn't shoot the first shot then he might not be strong enough to do that."

In even more grisly detail, Smyth continued, "They didn't talk about shooting the father a whole lot. They did say that they had to keep shooting their mother and they kept shooting her because she didn't move and they thought she might have lived."

Prosecutors and defense lawyers would not comment on Smyth's account. In the interview, Smyth said Oziel wanted her to listen in so that she could call the police if the conversation turned "violent ·or dangerous."

(If Smyth's statement that Oziel requested her presence in the next room is true, Oziel could be denying it because such a request for a third person to listen to a doctor/patient session without the consent of the patient could be considered highly unethical. The October 31st session was not tape recorded. It was only on December 11, 1989 — when the boys began to suspect that the police were suspicious — that Oziel taped the alleged "voluntary" confession. In that tape, it is said, the boys spoke of remorse and talked about psychological — but not sexual — abuse of both brothers.)

In her closing remarks on the television program, Smyth revealed that the brothers had indicated that the crime was really directed at their father.

"One of the things that I heard Lyle say, that was really disturbing to me, was 'For once, my father would have to congratulate me and give me credit that I planned the perfect murder. I carried out the perfect murder.'"

From apparent statements on the tapes, and from people who knew the family, there appears to be more than money involved in the alleged parricide. Lyle and Erik appear to have harbored a deep-rooted hatred for their parents — particularly Lyle for his father. Erik was closer to his mother.

An acquaintance close to the case and the family said the ugly word "incest" could crop up during the trial as part of the defense strategy. The same source told us that the boys were mere pawns in their father's dark side.

Even more damaging, someone who had knowledge of the contents revealed, "If they [the tapes] are ever released by the court, they will relate a great deal of psychological abuse by Jose on both brothers, but not enough to cause such violent retribution." Judalon Smyth, throughout several interviews, said she had never heard any statements about sexual abuse while in the adjoining office, nor did Oziel ever mention it to her during their relationship.

Investigators had been canvassing gun shops from Beverly Hills to the Mexican border for months in an attempt to find any paper work, compulsory under Federal statutes, of the purchase of any twelve gauge shot guns around March of 1989. Another break in the case occurred with the discovery that two such weapons had been purchased at a Big Five Sporting Goods store in San Diego.

Allegedly, Erik Menendez drove down the coast to San Diego two or three days before the tragedy and purchased two 12-guage Mossberg shot guns and two kinds of ammunition — large pellets and bird shot. Since the law required picture identification, Erik allegedly presented the driver's license of a Princeton friend of Lyle's, Donovan Jay Goodreau. Both men were similar in appearance. Goodreau managed to prove that he had been in New York on the day of the purchase, but told investigators that his driver's license had been "lost" several months before.

The scenario was perfect for a television movie. Following the startling developments, the rush to secure the story rights created a virtual stampede, setting new standards even for the well-known Hollywood hustle and fast buck operators. Because the victims had traveled among the elite of the film and music industries, the mystery in Hollywood's own back-yard spawned a wealth of rumors. Within a few weeks, very quietly, movie and book deals were being floated.

But the real rush to secure the rights to the murders

on Elm Drive followed the arrest of the brothers, Lyle and Erik.

One of those attempting to put together a deal was an actress-turned-producer, Karen A. Lamm. A self-described confidante and aerobics buddy of Kitty Menendez, Lamm admitted in March that she had been trying to package a television movie on the murders since mid-December. The questions asked of her by Beverly Hills investigators made her suspicious, even then, about the sons and their possible parricide.

An aspiring screenwriter and friend of Erik's from Calabasas High School, Craig Cignarelli, would add a grisly note to the proceedings. Erik and Craig once wrote a sixty six page screenplay about "the perfect murder." The screenplay—which Kitty Menendez helped to type—contained an early scene which contained the slaying of the main character's wealthy parents.

A blueprint for murder?

The arrests ended the ordeal and expense LIVE and Carolco incurred trying to get to the bottom of the murders. As police investigators and the media sought clues to the Menendez murders, both organizations had received close scrutiny. Both were known to have extensive and very complex business dealings around the world.

Their expenses included hiring two prestigious law firms to investigate the possibility of a "mob hit." A LIVE spokesman refused to comment on the results of the internal investigation by the law firms. Neither changed the course of their business practices as a result of the killings or the investigations. In 1991, Carolco had tremendous financial success with *Terminator II*.

Since the death of Menendez, however, Andrew Vajna and Mario Kassar have, to a great extent, severed their business relationship. Kassar now runs Carolco in a flamboyant and entrepreneurial fashion resented by many of the Hollywood community. Under Kassar, Carolco spent over $75 million on *Terminator II* — but reaped three times that at the box office. The company has also been known to pay seven figures for original screenplays from such writers as Joe Ezsterhaus. This *largesse* has upset many members of the industry, especially executives such as Jeffrey Katzenberg, production chief at Disney/Touchstone, who wrote a well-publicized memo in late 1990 complaining of the "excesses of the industry and its blockbuster mentality" that "more is good."

The outcome of the Menendez brothers' trial will probably not be known until sometime late in 1992. The defense, as part of its strategy, was willing to forego a preliminary hearing and go directly to trial in July of 1991. But the prosecution objected. District Attorney Ira Reiner noted that a decision on the admissibility of "key evidence" — the tapes — was still pending before the Supreme Court of California.

The prosecutor, Deputy District Attorney Pam Ferrero, told the Judge that if a preliminary hearing was waived by the Court, she feared that the defense would exercise its right to a "speedy trial." Such a hearing could take several months and could have forced prosecutors to try the case without the crucial tapes, evidence it considers "vital" to its case.

Possibly the prosecution views the tapes as the only solid evidence of the brothers' guilt, and that the evidence of the shotgun purchases is not strong enough.

What was the real motive for the killings?

Why have the police been unable to locate the murder weapons? What happened to them?

Was there psychological and sexual abuse to the brothers by Jose Menendez? He was known as a "do it right" father who pushed both boys relentlessly. He would keep Erik on the tennis court for hours at a time practicing. Menendez insisted that both "be the best" in everything they did.

Lyle was a big disappointment to his father because he was suspended from Princeton for cheating. All the ministrations to Princeton from his persuasive father could not overturn that one year suspension.

Did both brothers resent the philanderings of their father with other women because of the effect it was having on their mother? Was this part of the psychological abuse to which people and friends refer?

Only time will tell.

On publication of this book, Lyle and Erik will have been in jail without bail for almost two years without their guilt or innocence having been decided. The murders of Jose and Kitty Menendez are just two more bizarre and aberrant occurrences of people caught up in the heartless cyclone created by the excessive money, glamor and power of the Hollywood entertainment industry.

CHAPTER SEVEN

Sexual Harassment in Hollywood

*"To get to the top you need to 'boff' as many
people as possible. The key to succeeding
in this town is to do it with everyone
you can get in touch with."*
— **Kirstie Alley**

"He said 'I'll see that you never work
in this town again,' but it didn't deter me!"

The actress has since gone on to success in the long
running *Falcon Crest* television series and a range of
bigger and better roles, but her vivid memory still
recalls the threat made just after she had arrived in
Hollywood.

"I went to interview for another series with a man
who was a big name, a reputable producer—or so I
thought," she continues. "He said he liked me. He
brought me back three times to read and said I was
perfect for the part. The last time he brought me back,
he closed the door. We were alone. He started out with
that old cliche which has been used hundreds of times
in movies—and in offices. I told him I didn't like him
'that way.'

"With that he turned on me and threatened me about never working again."

Far more outspoken about the situation is *Cheers* co-star Kirstie Alley, who will earn at least $11 million in 1991 and 1992. Her salary from *Cheers* is estimated to be around $3 million. In addition, feature film work will bring in several more million. She is also the spokeswoman for a major cosmetic company.

Alley hates 'the producer's couch,' which she describes as a necessity in Hollywood. "Any would-be star *must* sleep their way to the top, or *should be prepared* to sleep their way to the top," she states, adding "this goes for males, as well."

The outspoken star believes that "to get to the top, you need to 'boff' as many people as possible," especially producers, who have the final say on who gets what part. "The key to succeeding in this town is to do it with everyone you can get in touch with," she admits.

Sexual harassment in other industries has been a constant focus of civil rights. The persuasive problem has resulted in sexual harassment law suits throughout the country and has been splashed across newspaper headlines and television broadcasts, digging behind the closed doors of multi-billion dollar businesses and senate sub-committee hearings. Many of the cases have resulted in heavy damages; at least one in a potential jail sentence for a major sports star.

"In Hollywood, you sue — you're through," stated a producer well-known for his casting couch conquests when we quizzed him about harassment and why suits are seldom brought against individuals or companies in the industry.

In Hollywood, the exploitation of women — some of the most beautiful in the world hoping for careers in films or television — is accepted as a matter of fact, the cost of doing business, so to speak.

The practice is not limited to the top of the heap. Often, the harassment comes from lower echelon workers, including crew members.

Recently, on the set of a Top Ten television series, a crew member cornered a young actress in the corner of the set, grabbed at her blouse to look at her breasts and fondled them — like an adolescent on a school bus. The set was in a "take" situation and the actress could not speak out. Finally, when the scene was in the can, the crew member made pointed comments about the actress "sleeping her way to the top," making sure as many people as possible could hear him.

Although a producer on the series reported that the man had been reprimanded, he was still measuring and pulling focus for the camera crew several weeks later.

In any other industry, such as an aircraft plant, an insurance office, or a law office, the girl could have filed a law suit against the employer and probably won heavy damages. But if any actress should file a claim — or even complain about her treatment — she would be labelled a "trouble maker," have her availability "flagged" in casting offices and seldom work again.

Stuntwoman and actress Jean Coulter arrived for

work on a Spelling/Goldberg Productions television pilot believing she had a job as a stunt driver—a job which involved "heavy car work" she had been informed by her union.

What she got, according to her later complaint, was a stunt coordinator who fired her when she refused to go to bed with him. Prior to her law suit, Coulter worked an average of 199 days a year for several years. Following the complaint, she worked 12 days in menial stunt work, mostly for non-union, independent producers.

To succeed in the brutalizing atmosphere of Hollywood, "starlets" (for want of a better term) must first survive by beating off those who wish to exploit them, and then find a way to use or outsmart the system.

"I spent a year, often standing in the snow for six hours waiting to read for thirty seconds to get a part as a bit player with one line," says actress Morgan Fairchild. "I know how easy it is to get lost in the shuffle. I've seen the manipulation, the abuse; I've seen them sleep with people who promise to push them ahead. I know how it feels to be treated like dirt."

Fairchild, originally from Texas, was a finalist in the "Miss Teen Age Dallas" contest at fourteen. Two years later, she modeled for a Neiman-Marcus catalog. When she moved to New York, she landed her first television role in *Search for Tomorrow,* a daytime soap opera. "I was smart enough to find a niche," she says. "They told me a good bitch was hard to find, and so I became a good bitch."

The "starlets" who do survive and have the best shot at success and longevity, are much like Morgan Fairchild. They have damned few illusions and realize that Hollywood operates like a business, not a dream factory. They do not kid themselves about becoming "overnight" successes. They realize that dinner with a producer will not automatically give them larger roles. Often, these girls with the matter-of-fact approach to success have grown up in Hollywood or on its fringes.

In a recent interview, Kirstie Alley related, "I think the industry in Hollywood is the most suppressive business on earth. Most people, even within the industry, are there to stop you and try to make you not succeed. Why? Because one day you might succeed them!

"If I wasn't working here and making a great deal of money, I certainly wouldn't live here. It's too spaced out, and it's also not the cleanest place in the world."

In recent years, Alley and husband, actor Parker Stevenson, reside in Hollywood only while they're working. In 1991, they purchased an estate in New England where they spend as much time as possible.

According to those who have succeeded, "street smarts," talent, good judgment, professional management, acting classes and a cash reserve are all required to achieve.

A consensus of those in the know indicates that even becoming the boyfriend, girlfriend or mistress of a powerful or influential person is no insurance to success. There are no short cuts to fame and riches in Hollywood.

Nevertheless, sexual harassment continues – not only inflicted on women by men, but on men by women, on women by women, and on men by men. Women who work as casting directors and agents harass beautiful young men, "byms" or "bims" as they are known in the underground language of telephone calls and person-to-person discussions of those on the prowl. One young actor told us, "I could have an acting job tomorrow if I gave in to the advances of a man who is in charge of the project."

One young actress went before the Grievance Committee of the Screen Actors Guild about a screening party at which a female casting director for whom she would be auditioning the following day put a hand on her leg and made it clear that, if the actress cooperated sexually that evening, it could "help her professionally."

"Everyone is afraid," says another actress who does not want her name used – for obvious reasons. "It makes people nervous just to talk about it, because, all of a sudden, you get branded as a troublemaker, and people don't want you around anymore."

Hollywood harassment extends even to the streets of Beverly Hills. One actress recalls a time when she had been in Hollywood for four months. She was walking near the Beverly Hills Hotel when a purple Rolls Royce forced her to the curb with hand signals. A swarthy man, shirt opened to his navel, heavy gold chains jangling as he walked, Gucci loafers on his feet, jumped out of the car and approached her.

"Ah!" he spoke in a heavy Mediterranean accent, "So, so beautiful. You know the magazine *Vogue*? I am putting you on the cover. Come and have dinner with me."

He then handed her a business card with a picture of himself and Sammy Davis, Jr. The actress thanked him politely and declined his offer.

The Screen Actors Guild has received numerous complaints about one phony who has been successfully peddling an imaginary movie role to aspiring starlets whom he meets in—of all places—supermarkets in Beverly Hills and West Hollywood. "This one particular guy has been going around town for three years," said a SAG official. "He tells a girl she would be perfect for the starring role in his movie and to meet him that night at his home for an audition. He then shows her a closet filled with negligees and tells her to pick the one that would be perfect for her character. He auditions her, tells her it's not good enough. 'You have to convince me,' goes the spiel. He plays the part of the leading man and begins kissing her," said the official, "and then, these girls end up in bed with him because he has been playing a very convincing role as a producer."

But the Screen Actors Guild says the problem lies not only with the phonies, but also with well-known, legitimate producers and agents, who have real power to hire. Most of those with that type of power wield it mercilessly. Young actors of both sexes frequently find themselves victims, even after they have gotten parts.

An actress, now twenty-four, told us, "I had a director come up to me and say he had some 'special work' for me at the wrap that day. He said he thought I would be perfect. What it turned out to be was a bra-and-underwear scene on the floor with whipped cream all over me."

"I looked at him and said, 'Please, don't insult my intelligence.' He just walked over to somebody else on the set — some little girl who didn't know any better."

Another young actress recalls the making of an NBC pilot: "I had worked about seven days and the director had kind of been flirting with me. By the middle of the shoot, he was adamant that he wanted to take me out that night. I had been in a relationship for more than seven years; I wasn't about to go out with anybody else. I turned him down very politely explaining my situation and loyalties.

"The next day he made my life miserable; he screamed at me in front of everybody. It was awful."

Needless to say, she has never worked for the director again.

On a recent radio talk show, another actress said that she was working on one of last season's new series (which is still running) and had been sexually harassed by the series star. "He began," she explained, "with remarks such as 'Who are you sleeping with?' and 'Is that how you got the job?'

"A few days later, it was suggestions: 'How about a hug?' first, then he suggested we take a walk together. And then he grabbed me—which I didn't like. I asked him not to and he replied, 'I just want to touch you!' I wouldn't let him."

Even then, she said, the advances continued. He said he would be at her house later for "dinner and a massage." The actress said she just walked off the set. The next day, his harassment continued. "He pushed me into a stage closet—which I couldn't believe! He told me, 'I want you. Help me make it through this day.'"

Her response, she told the host, was to refuse his advances and walk out of the closet, leaving him behind. But the star still would not quit making advances. She refused another demand that they have dinner.

"When I got home, I received a call," she said. "The word has come down. He doesn't want you on the set."

She had been fired.

Actress Tracy Scoggins' experiences on a segment of *Magnum, PI* several years ago had a similar outcome.

"We were shooting in Hawaii," she says. "My mother was with me and this actor who was guest starring kept hounding me and teasing me about my mother. One day I was swimming near my hotel when he approached me in the water and started grabbing and touching me.

"I tried to fend him off, and then, finally, I just slugged him. That night he purposely delayed my scenes and never found time to do them. The next day I was sent home."

Scoggins only related the incident for the first time much later in a major magazine because, she said, "I was told people would say I was a tattletale and that I would never work again."

But still they migrate to Hollywood: from New York, Des Moines, Chicago, Dallas or wherever. They are compelled by their very nature: an innocence and capacity for wonder, a hunger for fame, a place in the sun. They are searching for their fifteen minutes of fame, spurred by their need for risk and adventure and their belief that they can make it.

After appearing in high school or college plays for which they receive plaudits from their contemporaries, they feel they are ready for Hollywood. This is precisely why most of them fail. Only the standards and resources of Hollywood—and a great deal of luck—will provide them a way to success. Hollywood is not a high school or college drama department. It is a cold, ruthless business—not for the weak of heart.

The casting couch and sexual harassment have been going on since the establishment of the industry, and it will continue as long as aspiring young actors and actresses continue to sacrifice everything for their chance at the brass ring. One in a million may grab it.

The others haunt the streets, full of heartbreak, turning tricks for the Hollywood types cruising Sunset Boulevard, too ashamed to go home to Muscatine, Miami, or Kansas City and admit that they failed.

CHAPTER EIGHT

The Unsolved Murder of Karyn Kupcinet

"The seven death threats she sent to herself was one of the many strange things Karyn Kupcinet did to keep Prine from breaking off their relationship."
— Lt. Al Etzel
Deputy, Los Angeles County Sheriff

The nude body was found on Saturday night, November 30, 1963, on the couch of her West Hollywood apartment at 1227 N. Sweetzer Avenue. Lying a few blocks off the Sunset Strip, the residence was in an area of reasonable rents and easy access to agents' offices on the Strip.

The body of Karyn Kupcinet, daughter of Chicago columnist Irv Kupcinet, was discovered by actor Mark Goddard and his wife, Marcia. They had become concerned when they had found newspapers for three days on the landing outside the door of the second story apartment, topped by a dog-eared copy of Henry Miller's *Tropic of Capricorn*.

When there had been no answer to the doorbell, the Goddards had tried the door and found it unlocked.

"We called her name and thought she might be asleep because the TV was on, but there was no sound," said Goddard. Then they turned on the lights and saw her body.

It was around eleven p.m.

A stuffed pink and white panda bear lay near a capsized coffee pot. A lamp was overturned on the floor and, nearby, lay a brandy snifter, containing some filter tipped cigarettes. Other cigarettes were spilled across the floor.

A bathrobe was tossed across a chair.

Upon viewing the death scene, in revulsion the Goddards rushed downstairs and notified another tenant, Jack La Velle. La Velle, an advertising magazine editor, immediately called the West Hollywood Sheriff's office.

Because of the discoloration of the body, Sheriff's deputies were unable to determine immediately if there were any marks of violence. Mark Goddard told the police, "Karyn had dinner with us in our home last Wednesday night, Thanksgiving eve, and we haven't been able to get in touch with her since then." Both Goddards told the press "Karyn was very happy and vivacious the last time we saw her. She's not the sort of person who would commit suicide."

The coroner estimated that Karyn had died sometime early Thanksgiving morning. Because of the decomposition of the body, an exact time could not be determined. The autopsy revealed the cause of death as a broken Hyoid, the u-shaped bone at the root of the tongue. Originally stating that her death was due to strangulation by a left-handed person, the coroner was later to revise his statement.

Deputies investigating the scene noted no notes or empty pill bottles in evidence anywhere near the body. Dishes in the kitchen had been washed and were on the drain board. Because of the absence of clothing in the vicinity of the body, deputies assumed that the victim had known her murderer. The only clothing in the living room beside the bathrobe was a torn t-shirt.

Karyn Kupcinet had rented the attractive, four room apartment about three months before her death. Situated in a court of eighteen apartments in a two story, white Spanish style building, it was one of a group of comfortable units which were either rented or leased by motion picture and television performers and middle level executives.

A beautiful girl, Karyn was born on March 6, 1941, the daughter of famed Chicago columnist, Irv Kupcinet, and his wife Esther ("Essie") Solomon Kupcinet, the daughter of a prominent and wealthy Northside Chicago family.

After attending exclusive private schools on the east coast and graduating from Wellesley College, Karyn defied her parents' wishes and enrolled in the Actors Studio in New York to study under Lee and Paula Strasberg. She made her professional acting debut in 1954 in the Chicago production of *Anniversary Waltz* and appeared with Pat O'Brien and Joe E. Brown in stage versions of *Father of the Bride*.

According to reviews, she had excelled in twenty-six

segments of Gertrude Berg's television series and worked with Linda Darnell. She had finally received billing in a Jerry Lewis film, *The Ladies Man,* and drawn critical raves in a Laguna (California) Playhouse production of *The Miracle Worker.* Following a role in a Perry Mason episode just a few weeks prior to her death, *The Hollywood Reporter* said that Karyn, was "born to be an actress."

In his final report, the coroner reported that Karyn had been strangled with a great deal of violence, but had not been raped. While it appeared she had been strangled by a left handed individual, more than one hand was necessary to snuff out the life of the vibrant, young girl. The dishevelled condition of the apartment indicated a struggle with her attacker.

Because Karyn was nude, and since there was no evidence of forced entry, it was believed that Karyn knew her murderer. It was established that she was not in the habit of leaving her door unlocked. Other tenants reported hearing or seeing nothing unusual.

Jerry Lewis, with whom she had worked in several scenes of *The Ladies Man,* told investigators that "Karyn was a vibrant young kid and making an admirable go of it as an actress." On the other hand, he pictured her as a neurotic young woman entangled in a hopeless romance.

Police would later reveal that Karyn had composed seven death threats to herself with words cut from movie and fashion magazines taped to sheets of white writing paper. In investigating the notes, police found a fingerprint on the *underside* of a piece of the transparent tape used to secure the words to the paper. It was identified as the print of Karyn's own right middle finger.

Karyn had attempted to use the notes to bolster a sagging romance with a promising young actor, Andrew Prine. At the time of her death, Prine was the star of the television series *The Wide Country,* a story of vagabond rodeo performers. Although he had discounted them as the work of a crackpot, Prine had kept the notes after Karyn had given them to him. He later turned them over to Captain Al Etzel while he was being questioned.

Etzel said later he believed the notes to be one of the devices Karyn attempted to use to keep Prine from breaking off their romance. Prine revealed that on November 27th, a few hours before the murder, Karyn had called him and told him that someone had left a baby on her doorstep. Prine said that she sounded upset and he had told her to call the police. Because she had sounded unusual, he called her back about midnight after returning from a date with Hanna Capri, a television actress. Karyn told him that she had called the police and that they had taken the baby away.

Sheriff deputies investigating the case estimated that Karyn Kupcinet was strangled to death shortly after this call.

Police from Los Angeles and the Los Angeles County Sheriff's Office both checked their records, but found no record of a baby's being turned over to police at that time. Prine also related to investigators that

Karyn had once posed as a magazine writer and had attempted to interview people about another girl Prine was dating at the time. Some, becoming suspicious, refused to talk to her.

Another bizarre revelation belied the background of the well-born daughter of the wealthy Chicago family. On November 10, 1962, Karyn had been arrested for shoplifting in a Pamona (California) department store. The arrest record showed a security guard had caught her with two books, *Tao,* worth $1, and *Genius,* worth $4.50, and a pair of green Capri pants valued at $10.40. She also had in her possession a sweater reportedly taken from another store. Karyn had pleaded guilty and paid a $150 fine.

On hearing of his daughter's death, Irv Kupcinet flew in from Chicago. Stricken with rage, he told the press and Lt. Norm Hamilton, who headed the investigation, that "Karyn had more friends than anyone I've heard of lately. They all loved her. Someone must know something."

Because of the coroner's opinion that a left-handed person had strangled Karyn, detectives checked out every southpaw acquaintance—without results. The manhunt extended to Northern California and the beach cities where male friends of Karyn was questioned extensively.

Lt. Hamilton, pressured by Irv Kupcinet, who had powerful political connections in Illinois, pulled out all the investigative stops in a desperate move to solve the case. Illinois Governor Otto Kerner and Chicago

Mayor Richard Daly both telephoned their California counterparts that they would like to see the case cracked "fast," regardless of the consequences.

Norm Hamilton would later inform us that he did not work "Chicago style." The scenario for the murder — as far as he was able to conceive it — was as follows:

On Thanksgiving evening, Karyn had dined with Mark and Marcia Goddard. On returning home around nine p.m., she was visited by a neighbor, writer Edward Rubin, 22, and actor Robert Hathaway, 24, of Coldwater Canyon. They were the last two known persons to have seen Karyn alive.

Hathaway told investigators that he happened to be in her neighborhood and saw Karyn walking around the block "getting some air," she told him. Karyn told him that Rubin was in her apartment watching an episode of a series to which he had contributed and invited the actor to join them. According to the actor, this was around nine thirty p.m.

The three watched television and sipped coffee until Karyn excused herself, saying she was tired, and retired to bed. The two men left the apartment together, taking pains to make sure the front door was locked behind them. According to Hathaway, the time was 11:15 p.m.

Two phone calls for the evening were confirmed. Prine said he had called Karyn at midnight in an attempt to straighten out their relationship. The autopsy showed that she was strangled not long after that call. An earlier call had come from her father while Rubin and Hathaway were still in the apartment.

The book, *Tropic of Capricorn,* had come from Rubin, who had climbed the stairs to Karyn's apartment on Friday to return it. When he received no answer to his ring, he had left the book on her doorstep.

On a memo pad by her telephone, Karyn had kept notes on her conversations which led Hamilton and his crew down many paths, none of them productive. "We've chased our tails off," sighed one cop. "I'm beginning to think that this is a case of B&E (Breaking and Entering) with a robbery or rape that never happened as the motive."

There has not been a break in the case for twenty nine years.

Backstage at the Oscar Ceremony in 1976, almost thirteen years after the crime, Irv Kupcinet confirmed what investigators have always considered a strong possibility: that Karyn knew her killer, that her killer had a key to her apartment, or that she admitted the killer herself. In a national magazine article several months after her murder, Kupcinet said, "Even without a motive being established, we have a good idea who did it, but nothing we can prove."

But, in a bizarre way, the loss of Karyn's young life was not the only tragedy resulting from her death. Of all the friends to whom her father referred, the one who has suffered the most has been Andrew Prine.

In 1963, Prine appeared to be heading places and was much in demand. Apart from co-starring in *The*

Wide Country series, he was co-starred or featured in several theatrical films: *The Miracle Worker, Company of Cowards, The Devil's Brigade, One Little Indian* and several others.

Prine was called to the West Hollywood Sheriff's station for questioning on the average of once a week for several months following the murder. When we queried Hamilton on the questioning, he simply stated that "Mr. Prine has been a cooperative witness and has helped us in every way he can."

But, as the weeks turned into months, it was discovered that the ties between Karyn and Prine were very strong. According to Detective Floyd Rosenberg, Karyn was importuned by Prine a year before her murder to allow a process server access to a television studio where he could serve Vince Edwards. At the time, Prine's ex-wife had filed a separate maintenance suit against the actor and begun to date Edwards. Prine had filed a cross complaint and sought $250 per month from his ex-wife for support. Edwards' lawyer represented the ex-Mrs. Prine in Los Angeles Superior Court and labeled Prine's suit as "outright extortion."

Because of the process server incident, it was noted that the ties between Karyn and Prine were *very* close and that he could get her to do his bidding.

After Karyn Kupcinet was murdered, and Andrew Prine's close relationship with her became public knowledge, his world crumbled. Many of the columnists who had praised him as an up and coming member of the profession and had hyped him for stardom turned vicious.

Even though the police publicly vindicated Prine of any complicity in the death, gossip continued to link his name to the tragedy—and does to this day. His life has never been the same. A cloud still hangs over him and his name seldom appears on screen or television credits anymore. He has continued to work, but parts have become much smaller and the productions non-union, or fringe productions. The last visible credit was for the 1986 *Eliminators*.

As a result of the stigma, he became a prisoner of self-imposed isolation. "I would report for work and go straight home. I retreated—which was, perhaps, some sort of cowardice." He adds that he still bears the scars from the treatment he has received at the hands of several columnists. "I remember when Walter Winchell called me up shortly after Karyn's death. When I told him I didn't want to talk about it, he replied—and I'll never forget his exact words—'If you don't talk to me, I'll skin your ass!' And he did. I got a lot of bad raps in print for over a year from Winchell. He was also a close personal friend of Karyn's father."

Prine added ominously, "This is a strange business and even stranger town; it has a high mortality rate."

The murder of Karyn Kupcinet has never been solved—nor is it ever likely to be. While Irv Kupcinet and the police believe they know who killed her, they have never been able to prove it.

As in many another unsolved Hollywood murder, relatives or close friends, and, often, even the police, claim to know the murderer or murderers, or cause of death, but, lacking proof, are powerless to act.

There will be many more in the future of Hollywood the Bizarre.

CHAPTER NINE

"Erotomania" or Hollywood Stars Under Siege

"We did not step in until the last letter arrived which sent the actor up the wall. The package contained half a dozen razor blades with blood on them, a used sanitary napkin, and a used condom . . ."
— **Captain Dan Martin**
Threat Management Unit, L.A.P.D.

Stars of films and television, and even featured performers, are fair game in today's violent climate. They are stalked, harassed and threatened on a daily basis. One, Rebecca Schaeffer, has been shot in cold blood. Another, Theresa Saldana, was almost killed when her throat was slashed.

Such sordid events are far more prevalent than reported in the daily press. Los Angeles today is the most dangerous place in the world for both visitor and resident. The Los Angeles Police Department, as well as those of surrounding communities, has totally lost control of well-armed street gangs, whose illegally obtained armament is the envy of many small nations.

Because of the extremely high industry profile, wherein faces are seen in millions of homes across the country and in theatres every day, Los Angeles is involved in a form of terrorism, proliferating to an extent that the Los Angeles Police Department, in 1989, formed the Threat Management Unit (TMU) with its own trained squad of detectives. TMU advises celebrities how to protect themselves, essentially by working with private security firms, whose clients feel their lives might be in danger.

Of necessity, stars and lower echelon celebrities are taking up firearms and detailed instructions as to how to protect themselves from their own "fans." Protection methods have gone well beyond a ten-foot high fence (where such a height is legal) around their homes and video cameras trained on the front and back of their properties. Telephones and FAX machines are carried in many cars and concealed weapon permits rest in glove compartments.

Utilizing bodyguards, self-defense techniques and security organizations' elaborate (and expensive) computer tracking of potential assailants, celebrities are prepared to make sure they do not pay the ultimate price for their appeal and high profiles. But it is impossible to protect everyone twenty-four hours a day.

The list of celebrities on both the Pacific Coast and New York who have been bothered by crazed fans reads like a Who's Who of television, film and the music industry. Justine Bateman and Michael J. Fox of *A Family Affair*; Sean Penn; Donna Mills of *Knots Landing*; Vanna White; Sharon Gless; Anne Murray;

Michael Jackson; Sylvester Stallone and David Letterman.

Others include Christina Applegate of *Married — With Children*; Farrah Fawcett; Roseanne Barr and her husband, Tom Arnold. French star Catherine Deneuve was left bloody and shaken after a "fan" threw a rock through the windshield of her car.

World class names have been tragic victims. John Lennon was gunned down on the streets of New York. Theresa Saldana almost died when her throat was slashed by a crazed Scottish criminal and drifter who was in the United States illegally. Late night talk show host, David Letterman, has been harassed by the same woman for over seven years. Margaret Ray had delusions of being Letterman's "wife" and repeatedly broke into his home and drove his cars during periods when he was out of town.

Many others have not been publicized, especially male stars who have been troubled by homosexual males and female stars harassed by gay women.

Many of the obsessive fans are as well known as their victims: Mark David Chapman, who murdered John Lennon; John Hinkley, Jr., who shot President Ronald Reagan for the "love" of Oscar winner Jodie Foster; Robert John Bardo, who shot and killed television actress Rebecca Schaeffer; and Arthur Richard Jackson, who slit the throat of Theresa Saldana. Had it not been for the quick intervention of a water delivery truck driver, Saldana would have died on the spot.

The 1989 slaying of television actress Rebecca Schaeffer by Robert John Bardo served as a catalyst and a sobering wake up call for Hollywood. Schaeffer, a pretty, 21-year-old actress from Portland, Oregon, had barely penetrated the public's consciousness with her role in *My Sister Sam* when she was gunned down in the doorway of her comfortable Los Angeles apartment in the Fairfax district — an apartment whose ancient intercom system had been out of order for several months. Bardo merely pushed the button next to her name on the mail slots outside the front door.

Normally, through an intercom system to each apartment, an occupant could push a button to converse with the person on the doorstep. Rebecca was preparing for an audition with Francis Ford Coppola for a role in *The Godfather III* later that morning. She had recently returned from Italy after filming a mini-series on the Achille Lauro hijacking. Because of the faulty intercom, she ran down a flight of stairs to open the door. Before the pert, red-headed young actress could say a word, Bardo fired once into her chest, then turned and walked down Beverly Boulevard.

Bardo, at the time of the murder, was an unemployed native of Tucson, Arizona, who had last worked as a janitor at a Jack In The Box fast food restaurant. He had been writing Rebecca Schaeffer harmless love letters for months. He had also been writing to his sister in Tennessee, outlining his feelings for the actress:

"If I can't have her, nobody else will. I have an obsession with the unattainable and I have to eliminate something that I cannot obtain."

Bardo also threatened he would kill Rebecca Schaeffer unless she "saved her virginity" for him.

Few of the letters found their way to the actress.

Following their daughter's death, her parents said that she had seen several letters which were perfectly harmless, and then had forgotten about them. At the time, secretaries or production company personnel usually screened most such letters. Some they turned over to the addressee; others they simply threw away. Since 1989, if any are threatening in tone, or appear to impose an imminent danger, they are turned over to the TMU for analysis. In the past, this type of letter didn't mean much. But, in Rebecca's case, even though he never sent her a threatening letter, Bardo was deadly serious.

He learned her address through the simple expediency of paying a private detective agency, The Anthony Agency in Tucson, Arizona, to locate her. Bardo paid the agency $250 in cash to obtain the information for him. The interviewing investigator at the agency came forward as soon as he heard of Schaeffer's murder. Bardo, he said, had told the agency that he was an old friend of the actress and wanted to send her a present. To add to the deception, Bardo carried a glossy photograph of the actress with an inscription, "To Robert."

The agency, in turn, called upon a Los Angeles detective agency to run a check on Schaeffer's driver's licence at the Department of Motor Vehicles in Sacramento. Her address was obtained for the sum of

$5.00. Since the Schaeffer murder, these procedures have been tightened and information cannot now be obtained except by permission of the licence holder.

Early on the morning of July 18, 1989, Bardo wandered the streets near Schaeffer's apartment house for hours, carrying an 8x10 glossy photograph of the actress and asking people its exact whereabouts. More than one witness later related that he "seemed out of place" and "weird," but no one thought to call the police.

After loitering near the building, Bardo rang the buzzer to her apartment. As soon as Rebecca opened the heavy, glass and barred front door, he fired a penetrating wound into her chest.

His escape by Greyhound Bus to Tucson was only temporary. A tip from his sister led to his arrest the following day. His sister confided in a neighbor, a Tennessee Highway Patrol officer, that her brother was so obsessed with Rebecca Schaeffer that he used to kiss her face when it appeared on the screen. His bedroom, she added, was a "shrine" to the actress. As soon as she heard Rebecca had been shot, she recalled, chillingly, that her brother had called her just before the time of the shooting. He had told her that he was within one and a half blocks of the N. Sweetzer Avenue apartment. He had not mentioned that he intended to shoot Schaeffer.

The officer immediately relayed the information to Los Angeles detectives working on the case. Following Bardo's arrest, Tucson detectives, acting on the Los Angeles murder warrant, were stunned to discover that

Bardo had previously been in a mental institution after stalking another "Sam," little Samantha Smith. Smith, who visited the Soviet Union on a peace making mission and had appeared in the ill-fated Robert Wagner series, *Lime Street,* died tragically in a commuter plane crash. She had been returning with her father from a trip to London when the plane went down in a rain storm just two miles from her home airport.

One striking similarity tied the attacks on Rebecca and John Lennon together. Bardo, like Mark David Chapman, who earlier had killed John Lennon, was carrying a copy of J.D. Salinger's *Catcher in the Rye,* which he discarded before boarding the bus for Tucson. The murders of Lennon and Schaeffer were not the first perpetrated by individuals addicted to the Salinger book.

Bardo went on trial in late 1991 for the murder of Rebecca Schaeffer. Because of Bardo's agitated mental state, a pre-trial agreement between prosecutors and defense attorneys agreed that he would be given a life sentence, if found guilty, without possibility of parole.

To illustrate Bardo's highly agitated state, defense attorneys played a track from the album "Exit," by the Irish rock group, U-2. Bardo, they said, was addicted to the number, "The Joshua Tree." Immediately, Bardo started bouncing around in his chair, waving his arms and moving his body in time to the music, totally oblivious to anything around him.

Hollywood is in the business of illusions and artfully blurring the line that separates make believe and the real world. The week of Rebecca Schaeffer's death, however, the line became lost somewhere and police blotters were full of bizarre incidents:

- A man with a grudge and a gun smashed his way into Lorimar Studios, shot up a sound stage with the automatic weapon and then killed himself. A one time business partner of a featured actor in *Dallas,* he claimed a failed venture with the actor in the staple food of movie houses—popcorn. Before he shot up the studio, the man handed the guard an envelope that held a news article with the headline, "Dreams, Feuds, Love, Lawsuits—and Popcorn."

- A young "bit" actor, who once appeared on the *Chips* television series about two highway patrolmen who pursued and arrested criminals on Los Angeles freeways, was killed when a stolen Corvette being chased by Los Angeles police slammed into his car.

- Jasmine Guy of *A Different World* received a series of threatening letters from someone who described, in chilling detail, how he'd stood within ten feet of her at a party a few days earlier.

Comments about the week were varied.
"They talk about coincidences. They talk about

triad mythology, that disasters arrive in threes. They talk about the twin irritants of heat and humidity. Even the moon," said one Lorimar worker viewing the damage of the sound stage. "Well, it was a full moon last night. That's one explanation for it!"

"I think everybody in L.A. right now feels terrible. Everyone at the studio is talking about it," Theresa Saldana said in a statement given the day following Schaeffer's killing.

A radio performer remarked, "The city of L.A. itself—you've got people not only picking off high profile people in general, but just driving down the freeway, gang wars, people at fast food restaurants getting bumped off.

"There's a thin line anyway between fantasy and reality, and for people who live in a nether kind of world such as a movie, an actor or actress admired or reviled spurs something within them. Perhaps America's variegated cultures could possibly create a catalyst in some people for violence."

A psychologist who has written and produced several television movies, most notably *Miles to Go* starring Jill Clayburgh, sees the current swath of violence and threats against celebrities as another piece of the pattern without a pattern. "We have a society where frustration creates violence and where that violence intrudes on every level of life and life style.

"It has seeped even into the charmed circle of Hollywood as surely as it has in other parts of Los Angeles," he added.

The same psychologist commented that the man who killed Rebecca Schaeffer "probably fantasized an intimate relationship with her, which is borne out by his 'save her virginity for me' statement in the letter to his sister. What happens with television is even the people who are too psychologically weak to go outside and relate to people, can relate to people on the tube. Then, if it goes far enough, you get the Hinckleys and Jacksons (Saldana's attacker) who probably feel very self righteous in what they did."

In other words, anyone on television, young or old, is vulnerable to individuals like Jackson, Bardo, Hinckley or Chapman. The intrusion of real life on Hollywood is, of course, not new, but it does seem to many—the industry and security experts in particular—to be escalating every day.

This personalization, so to speak, with a performer has taken a bizarre turn. Several months before the death of Michael Landon, two Universal Studio front gate security guards refused to allow a man admittance to "meet his idol (Landon)." He killed both of them.

Security Consultant Gavin de Becker, who purposefully maintains a low profile, had been, and is, a security advisor to Theresa Saldana, Michael J. Fox and other Hollywood stars. He has conferred with legislators about special security problems for celebrities.

"There is," says de Becker, "a blurring of the line" of behavior toward stars that we come to feel intimately involved with — characters we really don't know, but think we do.

"When you look at the American Dream, this is the flip side," he sighs. "When they tell you you'll be famous and well to do — well compensated — they don't also tell you that you'll be at the center of a hurricane of very desperate people."

Psychologist Jerry Clark points out the need to reduce the amount of violence on television and in films. "Let's really face facts. Who really needs a *Lethal Weapon II* and a *Lethal Weapon III*? Who needs a *Godfather III* or a *GoodFellas,* with all its gratuitous violence. We could go on and on. Who needs 'true life' cases of violent kidnappings of peaceful citizens from Sleepy Hollow, U.S.A. with the wife being raped, beaten and shot and the husband thrown from a speeding car?"

The medium, as broadcast scholar Erik Barnouw once noted, has indeed become "the environment and context of our lives."

Following Rebecca Schaeffer's death, the Conference of Personal Managers held an "Artists' Protection Seminar" that attracted more than 300 managers and agents, representatives of the biggest names in the entertainment business. The seminar made public the information that Schaeffer was not the only one to suffer at the hands of a crazed "fan." Until the seminar, the statistics had been kept under wraps.

"More than half [the participants] reported some dealings with obsessed fans. That brought it home to us," said one agent. "Individually, none of us realized how prevalent it really was and is. It could even be more prevalent."

Immediately, the Los Angeles Police Department formed TMU, headed by Captain Dan Martin, a veteran detective. "The focus of the unit is on obsessive behavior over a period of time, as opposed to neighbors saying to one another, 'I'll kick your ass if it happens again.'

"We are not in the business of predicting violent behavior. We are all capable of violent behavior given the right 'hot' button."

What the TMU personnel attempt to do is "evaluate and attempt to predict the possibility of an encounter occurring." They keep track of correspondence between personalities and "fans" in a computer. Martin says the TMU, since its establishment, handled more than 100 cases through the middle of 1991, and has been successful in obtaining the identity of most of the "fans" writing the letters.

The TMU, however, does not contact every one. "As a rule, intervention makes things worse," says Martin. The unit is in constant contact with a trained psychologist and one officer is in a doctoral program to become a psychiatrist.

The squad will, however, make personal contact with an obsessed fan when certain patterns occur that indicate their behavior has moved to another, more violent level. Martin cited for us the case of a well-known television actor who had received hundreds of letters.

"They were filled with 'I love yous' but there were also statements that would concern anyone, let alone a cop," Martin related. "One letter read, 'Someday we'll get our body parts together in another universe!'"

The letters also provided contradictory clues as to where they had originated. They were written in red ink on Houston and Dallas newspapers. The postmarks, however, came from Ohio. The TMU monitored the letters, but had no intention of contacting the writer, even though they had discovered the writer's identity through cooperation with postal inspectors.

"We did not step in until the last letter arrived, which sent the actor up the wall and disgusted us, even though we are all 'hard boiled' cops. The letter-package contained a half dozen razor blades with blood on them, a used sanitary napkin, and a used condom."

Martin's unit stepped up the investigation.

The letter writer turned out to be a female college student from Michigan. She was warned to 'cease and desist' or face a felony prosecution. She did.

The ends to which these so-called "fans" will go, however, are myriad. Not all of them desist.

- Over the past decade, a 52-year-old farmer has been convicted eleven times of harassing Anne Murray. In 1989, he called her office 263 times in a six-month period.

- In 1988, an escaped convict, Daniel Vega, stalked Donna Mills. After a brief chase, police cornered

Vega's car near Pasadena, California. Instead of surrendering, he came out with guns drawn and was killed by police.

- Vanna White was once repeatedly stalked by a man identified as Roger Davis. Wearing a camouflage outfit and army dog tags—although he had no connection with the armed forces—Davis jumped out of the audience during the taping of *Wheel of Fortune* and claimed a former boyfriend of White's was a 'bad man' who was associated with "the Mafia." Davis, who still insists he will marry White, has frightened her into obtaining a restraining order, even though most recipients ignore them.

- Illustrating that it is not always strangers who menace actors, The *Young and Restless* star Thom Bierdz was forced into hiding when his younger brother Troy vowed to kill him. Thom had reason to fear his sibling. Troy Bierdz had just been charged with beating their mother to death with a baseball bat.

- Victoria Principal was tracked down on location in Utah by a lovesick lunatic who telephoned her on the set of a television film in which she was starring and producing. She also received threatening letters from another male who included his photo. Police were never able to discover if the two men were identical.

- Christina Applegate, of *Married—With Children,* had no idea her innocent "chat" with a neighborhood carpenter would lead to trouble, but career criminal, ex-con Thomas Soto pursued the young actress relentlessly. When she didn't respond to his advances, he broke into her house, yelling "I'm going to kill you!" Neighbors heard her screams and called police, who nabbed the love sick carpenter. Undaunted, he dyed his hair red in an attempt to disguise himself as co-star Katey Sagal, but was nabbed by security guards at the studio gate.

- Stunning French film star Catherine Deneuve was driving down a narrow street in France on a summer afternoon when her car windshield was smashed with a brick by a "fan" screaming he could not live without her. "It was the most terrifying moment of my life," she told gendarmes after they subdued the attacker.

- Justine Bateman told friends she "felt like a caged animal for six months" before a love-obsessed "fan" from Houston, Texas, John Thomas Smetek, 39, was caught. He had been stalking her and had gained entrance to the theatre where Justine was scheduled to appear with the Berkeley Repertory Company. Screaming that he was going to commit suicide, he was holding a gun to his abdomen when police cornered him in the theatre. The man had been known to TMU for several months in connection both with Bateman and another prominent figure.

- Candace Bergen displayed her courage and caution one night when she noticed that she was being followed from the studio. Bergen had previously been briefed by security advisors as to how to handle the situation. The alert actress called police on her car phone and then drove to the police station, where her "shadow" was apprehended.

- Even the macho Sylvester Stallone lives in fear after receiving death threats while on location in Mexico for *Cobra*. Stallone discovered a deadly snake in his bed. The perpetrator was never found, but, ever since, Stallone has had a heavy payroll of bodyguards in addition to state-of-the-art security precautions around his Beverly Hills estate.

One particular mental institution patient is prominent on the list of the celebrity security forces. Prosecutors in Illinois have alerted coast authorities to the possible early release of a patient who has written letters about his delusions involving many stars.

An assistant state's attorney in Illinois said he mailed notices during 1991 to Los Angeles and Beverly Hills police and to forty show business figures, to warn them that they had been the focus of delusions by a mental patient, Ralph Nau. "I've received a response from every one of them," says Randall Stewart. "All are definitely concerned."

Nau, 36, confessed to the 1984 ax murder of his eight-year-old step-brother, but was acquitted when a judge ruled that he was unfit to stand trial, and that he had been unfit to confess to the murder, but had done so under duress.

Randall Stewart says that Nau has mentioned the celebrities in hundreds of letters to his family. Before his entrance into the mental institute, he followed Sheena Easton to Scotland and twice trailed Olivia Newton-John to Australia.

Nau also wrote his family that the stars composed songs for him, held benefit concerts for his "legal defense fund," built homes for him and asked him to enter into sexual affairs with them and sire their children. Stewart's list contained the names of Newton-John, Cher, Madonna, Vanna White, Mary Hart, Heather Locklear and others.

Olivia Newton-John was especially prominent in Nau's correspondence. He had traveled to Australia to tell her he believed she was being impersonated by an evil double, but could not make contact. He then journeyed to Las Vegas to seek out Cher.

In checking with the Los Angeles County District Attorney, it was learned that Nau used the alias "Shaun Newtonjohn" to obtain a California driver's licence in 1983.

The public defender who represented Nau in his murder case, and in the case which had him committed, said his client is "schizophrenic, delusional and has visions of grandeur," but is not dangerous. His statement is contrary to the gut feelings of all the security agents and TMU personnel with whom we discussed the problem.

What triggers people such as Bardo, Davis, Jackson and others to commit acts against celebrities?

The behavior is called "erotomania" and causes such people to focus on celebrities with an intensely felt "death wish." The term is applied by psychologists and psychiatrists when a disturbed person develops a romantic interest in a celebrity.

Newport Beach psychiatrist, Dr. Park Dietz, has made an extensive study on the problem for the National Institute of Justice. Nearly 95% of these "fans," according to Dietz, are mentally disturbed. The basis for his finding is from the study of approximately 5,000 letters supplied by Gavin de Becker among others.

Dietz did, however, discover that those who write letters filled with hate and threats of the worst kind are the least likely to attempt contact with the celebrities to whom they address their sick remarks. The letters to Rebecca Schaeffer were never threatening, only endearing. Dietz, who testified at Bardo's trial, discovered that delusional fans who write about romance and personal intimacy are the most likely to attempt contact.

Both Dietz and Gavin de Becker came up with another analytical finding which has helped immeasurably in understanding the "Delusional Fan": the celebrity need not be a major star—as in the case of Rebecca Schaeffer. In fact, Dietz's study stated that such persons are often intimidated by the mega-stars, whom they consider larger than life and unobtainable.

In Dietz's opinion, players such as Schaeffer and Olivia Newton-John—the typical "girl-next-door" types—are almost irresistible to crazed fans. In many cases, the "fan" is personally physically unattractive. Instead of forming real bonds with others like themselves, they fixate on those with superior status and looks. This, in turn, allows such "fans" to feel special, as if they've been plucked out of their ordinary worlds by special stars. As soon as reality sets in and they are spurned, they focus on punishing the stars responsible.

Unfortunately, such attacks on celebrities are on the rise. The Dietz study claims that, since 1968, there have been as many attacks as there were in the previous 175 years. One spokesperson at the Artists Protection Seminar believes the increase is due to "societal change where more and more people are alienated from life and reality."

De Becker argues that fan violence is due to the emphasis by the tabloids and television on the personal lives of celebrities. "Nowhere in history could you completely 'know' someone like you can Johnny Carson," de Becker emphasized.

Following Schaeffer's murder and the attack on Theresa Saldana, Hollywood is now taking all crazed fans very seriously—especially when they can be spotted or detected through "fan mail" opened by studio or agency personnel. Secretaries and other "letter openers" have been instructed to save all "strange" letters. Stars now live by a new set of rules. Some, such as Eddie Murphy and Prince, seldom leave home without being surrounded by bodyguards. Post office boxes, rather than home addresses, are listed on all official correspondence. Home telephone numbers are never released, although a lucrative, underground facility for obtaining such numbers exists through some "fan" clubs. Lately, such organizations have been very careful to whom they disseminate this information.

Messenger services are instructed to deliver scripts to agents' offices, never to stars' homes. The Department of Motor Vehicles now permits alternate addresses, such as post office boxes, on drivers' licences and automobile registrations.

Sharon Gless, the star of *The Trials of Rosie O'Neil,* had a particularly close call with a fan in April 1990.

The actress was not at her home in the San Fernando Valley when Joni Leigh Penn broke in, with the admitted intent to sexually assault the actress and then kill both Gless and herself.

Before being sentenced to a six year term for breaking into Sharon's home, Penn was an active and well known member of the Lesbian community of Los Angeles.

Armed with a semi-automatic rifle and more than 500 rounds of ammunition, the unattractive woman held a Los Angeles Police Department SWAT Team at bay for more than seven hours before surrendering. Police who arrested her said that Penn could well have shot Gless if she had been home. Gless had been using the house only as an office and had been staying at the home of her fiancee.

Penn broke into the house at 3:15 a.m., obviously hoping to catch Gless by surprise in bed. Instead, she triggered a silent alarm which brought two Los Angeles Police Department officers to the house within three minutes.

Gless was familiar with Penn, who had visited the "Cagney & Lacey" set many times. Michael Gless, the actress's brother and attorney, stated that, during that period, she had always seemed "well behaved." However, this was not the first time she had attempted a sexual assault on Gless.

According to police lieutenant Ron La Rue, "Penn had sent over 100 'obsessive' letters to her during the previous four years. She wanted to be near her." An earlier "visit" by Penn to Gless's home prompted Penn's psychiatrist to alert the actress that the "fan" intended to shoot herself in front of her. Gless obtained a restraining order.

At the time of the Restraining Order hearing, Sharon Gless remarked, "These are horrendous, dangerous times we live in, especially when disturbed people have such easy access to weapons that can be used indiscriminately."

While she was barricaded in the house, a trained police negotiator was brought in to talk to Joni Lee Penn. The negotiator was a man. This incensed Penn considerably and she told police she would not communicate "with a man." When a female negotiator was brought in, she surrendered.

At Penn's trial, Sharon testified, "I didn't think anything like this would ever happen — never in a million years." Under cross examination by Penn's Public Defender, Mitchell Bruckner, she added, "I don't think that way."

Bruckner disputed police accounts of Penn's crime and her intent. "She never intended to hurt the actress or steal anything," he told the jury. Penn had admitted to police that she had intended to kill Gless.

Gless also admitted on the witness stand that she and her public relations counsel had lied to the press that the Studio City home was an office because they both feared that she could be tracked down there by Penn. She admitted that, until the break-in, she spent about 70 percent of her time at the house. "I lied to protect myself since the press had blasted my exact address all over the newspapers."

Exposed as they are to the public, harassment by delusional "fans" is becoming a horrendous problem for celebrities. It is also becoming a tremendously expensive sidelight to fame. Bodyguards and security measures do not come from a bargain basement catalogue. They are the fastest growth businesses in Southern California — at least in 1991, and probably into 1992, according to de Becker and others.

Surprisingly, with the exception of Rebecca Schaeffer, Theresa Saldana and, of course, John

Lennon, no other stars have met with bodily harm. Several have come close.

Their personal safety—and that of their families—demands expensive security precautions around their homes and the studios where they work.

The computers at the TMU are filling with more data every day. Rumors also exist that some stars have had "homing" beepers implanted on their persons, similar to small pacemakers, so that authorities can trace them. Such a device is possible and is rumored to be in use in political circles.

Hollywood's system for protecting its human assets has always been limited, particularly since the end of the studio system. Hollywood's most valuable asset is people—the stars, featured players and supporting actors and actresses who enliven movie and television screens.

The wealthiest and most successful—the Stallone's, the Madonna's, the Beatty's, the Nicholson's—will always have the wherewithal to hire bodyguards and install security systems. They can hide behind walled estates, isolated by iron gates and wired shrubbery.

But for comers like Rebecca Schaeffer, unlisted telephone numbers and screening services are all that stand between them and violent, delusional fans.

This is something about which Hollywood, per se, should be very concerned. One never knows when another Robert John Bardo, an Arthur Michael Jackson, a Mark David Chapman or a Joni Leigh Penn will come down the turnpike armed with deadly weapons and with carnage on their mind.

All are far from being the "fans" they profess to be.

CHAPTER TEN

Jayne Mansfield— Satan's Slave

> *"Jayne Mansfield, alone, accounted for more
> than 450 performances of* Rock Hunter
> *and that's an enviable mark for any
> new star on Broadway."*
> — **Harry Brand**
> Publicity Director, 20th Century-Fox

On June 29, 1967, we were in Las Cruces, New Mexico on location with Clint Eastwood filming *Hang 'Em High* when we heard the news.

Coming down to breakfast, we were startled to hear a radio newscast announcing the death of Jayne Mansfield in a car accident on Route 91, known as the Old Spanish Trail, 20 miles east of New Orleans.

Jayne had been with her current lover, Beverly Hills attorney Samuel Brody, in the front seat of a large sedan with driver Ron Harrison, an employee of the nightclub where Jayne had been filling in for a friend. Three of her children and four Chihuahua dogs were in the back seat.

The family was heading for New Orleans where Jayne was scheduled for a television interview the next day.

Around midnight, a highway department truck was spreading a thick white fog of mosquito spray. Easing along behind the slow-moving truck was a huge, eighteen wheel, flatbed semi. The sedan, with Harrison at the wheel, Sam beside him and Jayne next to the door, came around a curve—and plunged into the chemical fog. Before Harrison could spot the semi in the thick haze, the heavy sedan slammed into its rear trailer with such force that the entire top of the car was peeled back. The three in the front seat were killed instantly as the Buick went under the flatbed. Jayne's children and the dogs escaped injury. The children had been asleep on the back seat, the dogs on the floor.

The impact sheared off the top of Jayne Mansfield's skull. Her long, blonde hair, still attached to her scalp, was seen on the hood of the wrecked sedan when pictures came over the Associated Press wire the next morning.

Several weeks before, during a circuit tour of Ireland, France and Sweden, Mansfield and Brody had engaged in a continual series of drunken fights and shattering rages, based on jealousy. We had been aware of the jealousy when we interviewed Jayne in her "Pink Mansion" on Sunset Boulevard a few weeks previously. Brody, aware that we had known Jayne for years, never left our sides during the interview. His jealousy of Jayne was well known and had made him a figure of ridicule around Hollywood.

Brody's estranged wife, Evelyn, a victim of multiple scherorosis, was in the process of suing Brody for divorce, accusing him of adultery with Jayne Mansfield. The divorce was pending while Brody, for all practical purposes, deserted his practice, supposedly to handle Jayne's business affairs and her pending divorce from Matt Climber, who was also accusing Jayne of committing adultery with the attorney.

The European tour had been a total disaster. The group had been asked to leave the Rose of Tralee Festival in Ireland when the Bishop of Tralee learned that Jayne was a practicing Satanist in an almost Catholic country.

In Stockholm, Jayne wound up sprawled on the dance floor of the seedy Afroskandia Club when she and Brody got into a fight over a remark about Jayne's charms.

Following the ill-fated European sojourn, the couple returned to Hollywood, and the "Pink Mansion" — very much a dejected pair. But there was yet another blow to befall Jayne.

Jayne's oldest daughter, Jayne Marie, then sixteen, welts and bruises on her body, walked into the West Los Angeles Police Station in tears. She told authorities that the short of stature, explosive-tempered Brody had inflicted them with a leather belt. Upon investigation, the family doctor claimed that Jayne had spanked her daughter "like any good parent." While an investigation was underway, Jayne Marie was placed in the protective custody of the Los Angeles County Social Services Agency.

With Jayne Marie's charges still pending, her mother agreed to a short engagement at a mangy Biloxi, Mississippi waterfront nightspot, Gus Stevens' Supper Club. Her show was a tawdry song and dance routine: a swift comedown for Vera Jayne Palmer, the buxom beauty from Texas who always wanted to be a top star, but never quite made it.

Buddy Adler, production chief at 20th Century-Fox, sensed Jayne Mansfield's movie potential when he and his wife, Anita Louise, saw her in *Will Success Spoil Rock Hunter* on Broadway. After a screen test at Fox's New York headquarters on West 54th Street, Adler purchased the rights to the play in order to secure Jayne's release from her Broadway contract. Jayne was signed at $2,500 per week and promised her original role in *Rock Hunter* when the film was made.

Her career was launched with *The Girl Can't Help It* in 1956, by far the best of the rock 'n roll musicals of the 50s cycle, followed by John Steinbeck's *The Wayward Bus*. Fox lived up to its promises, and the film version of *Will Success Spoil Rock Hunter* still stands as Jayne Mansfield's definitive film. After several more films for Fox under her contract, the Tropicana Hotel in Las Vegas offered her $25,000 per week for four weeks. Her career decline had started after only ten films.

Tropicana Holiday, in which she starred with husband Mickey Hargitay whom she married in 1955, was a fair success at the Tropicana. The review also starred George Chakiris and Cathy Crosby, Bob Crosby's daughter.

Comedian Tommy Noonan produced *Promises, Promises* and also co-starred with Jayne. Noonan shot two versions of the film. One was well-clothed enough for an American audience, while another version, with a great deal of Jayne shown alluringly in a bathtub, was intended for the more liberal European audiences.

Promises, Promises became what is known in the trade as an "art house" picture, or, even worse, a "jinx" film. Five people associated with the production died, either violently or by their own hands.

- Ann Thomas, the actress-wife of director King Donovan, died from an overdose of barbituates.

- Marie "The Body" McDonald, wife of co-producer Donald Taylor, died from a massive dose of drugs and alcohol.

- Two months later, Taylor himself committed suicide in the same room in which he had discovered his wife's body.

- In 1968, Noonan, 46, died of a brain tumor operation from which he never recovered.

- Jayne Mansfield was the fifth victim.

Mamie Van Doren, who later made *Three Nuts in Search of a Bolt* with Jayne and Noonan, was also featured in *Promises, Promises*. It was Van Doren who indirectly contributed to Jayne's death in Louisiana.

Not long after her third marriage to Matt Climber, Jayne was invited to a dinner party at Sammy Davis' home. Jayne was impressed with the Satanic Baphomet medallion the entertainer always wore around his neck. That night, Sammy Davis, Jr. introduced Jayne to another guest at the party, Anton LaVey, High Priest of the Church of Satan.

LaVey, born in 1930, had founded his church in 1966. He was known as a versatile and mysterious man who had worked as a circus lion tamer, a magician and a crime photographer for the San Francisco Police Department. He was known to keep a lion on the church premises and terrified his neighbors by walking the beast on residential streets.

San Francisco authorities had finally ordered him to remove the lion from the church, following a storm of protests from sedate area residents.

For some unknown reason, satanic services at The Church of Satan attracted a procession of Hollywood celebrities, including Sammy Davis, Jr., singer Barbara McNair, actor Keenan Wynn and Jayne Mansfield.

Following the Davis dinner party, and sometime during her marriage to Matt Climber, Jayne decided to abandon her Christian upbringing and join the Church of Satan. On a foggy night in San Francisco, one year before her death, she arrived at the already crowded "church."

Her induction was like a scene from a Vincent Price horror film. She knelt at the satanic altar and pleaded for a curse to be placed on Matt Climber, as black candles burned and the High Priest of the Church of Satan, Anton LaVey, held his hand on her head.

The liturgy started Jayne on strange "pilgrimages" to the "Devil House," as it was called by locals. But she no sooner got involved in the weird works of Satanism than hard times set in for her.

- Her marriage to Climber, which had produced a son, ended with his accusation of adultery with Brody.

- Her six-year-old son by Hargitay, Zoltan, was critically mauled by a lion at a Los Angeles wild animal park.

- After negative publicity about her satanic worship, 20th Century-Fox put Jayne on the shelf, cancelling her contract, but reserving the right to recall her.

Jayne hit the nightclub circuit and continued with her belief in LaVey and his church. In 1966, she asked the High Priest to "hang a curse" on Climber for trying to take custody of their child.

"After [Jayne] won a favorable court ruling [for the child's custody], she became an even more ardent Devil's disciple," reported Arthur Lyons in *Satan Wants You: The Cult of Devil Worship in America.* The fading actress also called LaVey for help after Zoltan was mauled, and the High Priest "summoned all his magical powers, while bellowing out a soliloquy to Satan," wrote Lyons.

Jayne credited LaVey with Zoltan's miraculous

recovery and swore her "undying loyalty to LaVey and the Prince of Darkness." Mansfield and Brody became regular visitors to the Church of Satan.

Brody, however, was not a member, and he and LaVey shared an intense hatred for each other. The animosity between the two men finally exploded into an angry showdown when Brody put his hand on a "holy" statue of a naked woman that stood at the altar of the church, sneering his admonition and blowing out several candles around the statue. When Brody threatened to expose LaVey as a phony, LaVey cast a curse on the attorney, told Brody he was "doomed," and threw him off the premises.

In the next eight or nine months, Brody was involved in eight automobile accidents, breaking an arm and a leg in one of them. The ninth accident was the fatal crash that killed all three in the car in Louisiana.

Many of Jayne's friends claim that Jayne, too, was stricken by Brody's "curse."

- Following Zoltan's miraculous recovery from the lion's mauling, he was diagnosed with spinal meningitis and was, once again, declared critical.

- The following day, Jayne was stricken with viral pneumonia.

- While on a trip to Japan, her treasured diamonds were stolen and never recovered.

- Soon after, in London, she was publicly humiliated and had to cancel a performance when she was accused of not paying a hotel bill—a serious offense in Britain.

- Returning home, she was hit with a charge of tax evasion by the Venezuelan government.

- Later, she was again robbed in Las Vegas and attacked at the Mardi Gras in Rio de Janeiro by a crazed mob who stripped her to the waist.

LaVey claimed that he had warned Jayne to steer clear of Brody for her own good, but she had ignored his warning. The two were never to speak to each other again. Later, LaVey blamed himself for Jayne's death, claiming that, when the telephone rang to notify him of her death, he had been clipping some articles from newspapers and magazines. As he laid them down to answer the phone, he noticed that, on the back of one clipping, he had cut off the top of a picture of Jayne.

Vera Jane Palmer, known to the world as Jayne Mansfield, was buried next to her father in Philadelphia. Her father had been a prosperous Main Line lawyer, who harbored a desire to be president. He had died when Jayne was three, devastating her.

The copper casket was draped with 500 pink roses with a large heart in the center. Mickey Hargitay, who always loved Jayne, struggled hard to maintain his composure. "Nobody really understood her," he said. "Nobody really knew the real Jayne."

One of the ironies of her death was that awaiting her at her home on Sunset Boulevard was a contract to star in the London stage production of *The Memoirs of Fanny Hill,* a stage play depicting the life of an 18th century English bawd. She had sought the part, keeping it a secret from Brody, whom she knew would object to her leaving the country. She was sure that returning to the stage, where she had been so successful in *Will Success Spoil Rock Hunter,* would get her career back on track.

A second irony was that Jayne did not want to make the Biloxi Supper Club appearance. As a favor, she had stepped in at the last minute for an ailing friend, Mamie Van Doren.

In 1980, Loni Anderson portrayed Jayne Mansfield in a television film based on the star's tragic life. With Arnold Schwarzenegger portraying Michey Hargitay, the film presented a distorted drama about Jayne's life in Hollywood.

At her peak, Jayne had a theory about her early success. "Shock," she explained. "It was shocking things that got me where I am today. That's why I'm a star.

"No one wants to see, or read about, a dull subject. I don't consider myself a dull subject."

Dull, she certainly was not.

We miss Jayne Mansfield—whether starring in a film, on the stage, or opening a supermarket. She was always "good copy." That's all any of us in the Hollywood press corps ever asked for. It was a sad return flight to Los Angeles from Las Cruces.

She is sorely missed.

CHAPTER ELEVEN

Hollywood's Blacklist Hypocrisy

*"I have been blackballed from
movie and TV roles because liberal producers
don't want me around!"*
— **Pat Boone**

In the last thirty years, Hollywood has been dominated by one mindset: it rejects anything remotely resembling mainstream or traditional values of American life. It has become intolerant of any views considered out of step by its ultra-liberal, left wing establishment.

For example, though there have been attempts to downplay its effect, the United Nations' "Register of Entertainers and Actors Who Have Performed in South Africa" stirs no animosity within the liberal ranks or its allies in most of the major news media in the United States, including the once middle-of-the-road *Los Angeles Times*—even though it is the closest example to a formal blacklist within industry ranks.

But it was the liberals and the communist sympathizers of the late 1940s and 1950s who screamed the loudest at the Hollywood blacklist of those who refused to answer questions before the House Un-American Activities Committee (HUAC).

Those who support that United Nations registry say it is not a "blacklist," but simply a record of performers who have violated the cultural boycott of South Africa. Just what business that organization has in poking its nose into show business we cannot understand. All anyone has to do to get off the list, they say, is to promise not to work in that country again.

Recalling the 1950s, all the Communists and fellow travelers in Hollywood had to do was to renounce their membership in the party or communist "front" organizations. Hollywood is still resentful over that list because some of the biggest names in Hollywood were on it.

Today, most liberals are still fighting the same battle, but say nothing of the United Nations Registry, which is tantamount of a blacklist of the 1990s. This has prevented a lot of performers, particularly nightclub performers, under threat of a total United States boycott, from earning any money in South Africa.

We could not believe it when, in December, 1990, a petition in the form of an advertisement signed by fifty screenwriters and producers appeared in the Hollywood trade papers. The petition demanded that Lorimar Studios remove the name of the late Robert Taylor from a building controlled by their organization on MGM studio property.

Taylor, the advertisement claimed, had "cooperated with the House Un-American Activities
Committee in 1947" and testified, under subpoena,
what he knew concerning Communist Party infiltration
of the industry that was extensive.

"What Taylor did destroyed careers," claimed Stan
Zimmerman, a Lorimar writer who organized the
petition. "The man named names pretty seriously. In
this age of Jesse Helms and other right wing noise-
makers," he puttered and stutter in an interview, "we
decided to take action."

Taylor, who starred in such films as *Magnificent
Obsession, Quo Vadis, Waterloo Bridge* and many other
top films, had been dead for more than twenty two
years. Hollywood seemed to be fighting ghosts.

Lorimar executives caved in to the demands, and,
almost overnight, renamed the building for director
George Cukor. With six series running on three
networks, it could not risk altercations.

Nearly everyone realized that Zimmerman was
following the fashionable industry political line that
was bound to keep him employed.

Robert Taylor was a top star and leading man and,
to those who knew him well, one of the most decent
people in the industry. Following his testimony, and at
the conclusion of his MGM contract, Taylor became
almost a non-person.

During his testimony before the house panel,
Taylor had referred to only three people by name — actor
Howard Da Silva, starlet Karen Morley and screenwriter
Lester Cole — and had never called them communists,

but had merely stated that he had heard they were communists.

At the time, Taylor was not only urged to testify by Louis B. Mayer, but was requested to do so by the studio. Karen Morley, the only one of the three surviving, admits that dozens of other Hollywood figures also labled her a communist during and after the 1947 meetings.

Following the change of name, Taylor's daughter, Tessa, stated that "Today it's easy to say he shouldn't have said anything, but the atmosphere was different then, and the hatred and fear of communism was real. Daddy spoke out for what he believed in. He can't defend himself now."

In an interview for the *Sacramento Union,* Roy Brewer, co-founder with Ronald Reagan of the Motion Picture Alliance, said, "Robert Taylor was a good, decent, patriotic American."

In 1947, a sub-committee of the House Un-American Activities Committee (HUAC) held preliminary hearings at the Biltmore Hotel in Los Angeles. Though the hearings were closed to the public and the press, Robert Stripling, the chief investigator, took care to inform the media of the charges made by the witnesses.

Stripling said Taylor had told the committee that United States government officials had prevented him from entering the navy in 1943 until he had completed *Song of Russia* for MGM. Taylor identified this picture as "communist propaganda that favored Russian ideologies, its institutions and its ways of life over the same things in America."

The film became an embarrassment to MGM when the political climate shifted following World War II. Taylor testified, on camera, in 1944, saying he had objected strenuously to doing *Song of Russia* at the time.

"I don't think that film should have been made. It wouldn't be made today," he testified. He added that he would not perform alongside communist actors. "If I was suspicious. . . it would have to be him or me." *Song of Russia* also starred Susan Peters and John Hodiak.

Edward Dmytryk is regarded as the most tragic figure of reverse historical revisionism and reverse McCarthyism created by the Hollywood liberal establishment.

Dmytryk was a top director in Hollywood, under contract to RKO-Radio Pictures and earning $2,500 per week—prior to the HUAC hearings. He is, today, one of only two surviving members of the "Hollywood Ten." After serving his prison sentence for contempt for refusing to answer HUAC questions, Dmytryk broke publicly with the Stalinists. Unable to find work in Hollywood, he moved to London and directed four films. After another in France, he returned to the United States and reestablished his career with films like *Alvarez Kelly, Bluebeard, The Caine Mutiny, Raintree County, The Young Lions* and *Anzio.* However, he had lost many years of a profitable and fruitful career.

Any doubts about the viciousness, vindictiveness and blind loyalty of the Hollywood left was erased when Dmytryk attempted to participate in a Spanish symposium in 1988 in Barcelona. Although he was the only member of the "Hollywood Ten" in attendance, other participants threatened to boycott the event if he took part in panel discussions.

Walter Bernstein, whose films *The Front* and *The House on Carroll Street* helped shape the views that many have about the blacklist period, told *Daily Variety,* "I said I wouldn't participate in this if Dmytryk were here. It's not a debatable subject."

Another well-known director, Jules Dassin, shared Bernstein's view. "I don't believe you enjoy your freedom," he was quoted as telling Dmytryk, who was relegated to sitting in the audience and enduring the insults of his colleagues.

This is still the mindset of Hollywood's liberal establishment, estimated to be at least 75 percent of the industry. Unfortunately, that 75 percent does all the hiring, firing, deal making, decision making and casting.

When Americans supported the black list of the "Hollywood Ten," they were essentially shunning traitors to the American way of life. Today, it is different; all success is based on left wing political orientation.

The late Lela Rogers, mother of Ginger Rogers, told HUAC that her daughter had refused to speak the line "Share and share alike, that's democracy!" in *Tender Comrade,* a film written by the leader of the *Hollywood Ten,* Dalton Trumbo. The premise of the film, a story of communal living by wives while their husbands were away at war, caused the HUAC to label it as "communist propaganda."

Mrs. Rogers was very outspoken about communists within the industry, especially at RKO, and identified Trumbo, as well as Clifford Odets, as communists. Two other members of the "Hollywood Ten," Adrian Scott and Joseph Losey, were also under contract to RKO. Adolph Menjou told the committee that "Hollywood is one of the main centers of communist activity in America."

In retrospect, the production of films like *Song of Russia, Tender Comrade, Mission to Moscow* and *North Star* was understandable. The United States was engaged in an alliance with the U.S.S.R. in a war against Hitler and Nazi Germany.Many, however, thought the propaganda written by writers like Trumbo and Odets went too far.

Meanwhile, committee staffers visited Hollywood offices, threatening producers to clean their houses of communists and communist sympathizers before they were compelled to do so by Congress and public opinion.

This was the climate of the "Blacklist" of the 1950s. Some of it was justified; some of it was not.

In the 1990s, it is very different.

The blacklisting of communists forty years ago was, as many scholars and historians have intimated, necessary. The list dealt with possibly treasonous anti-Americans and also included foreigners such as Hans and Gerhart Eisler and Bertolt Brecht, who were under contract to the industry.

The 1990s "word of mouth" *de facto* blacklist can and does prevent people from working because they supported Ronald Reagan, George Bush or other conservative political candidates. Recently, pro-lifers have felt they have suffered. In the last few decades, the country has tended to be divided among moral, rather than political lines. Susan Carpenter McMillan, director of the Right To Life League, insists that "Some of the biggest names in the industry have told me there is informal blacklisting against pro-life actors and actresses."

Pat Boone, Charlton Heston and Helen Hayes are among those who have expressed strong pro-life feelings. Almost without exception, the most active in the movement are not performers still in the process of building their careers. But even those with established careers and strong public identities can still fear the hand of this decade's blacklist.

Where are the outspoken liberals who say nothing about this current unofficial "blacklist" which is depriving many people of their living, but are still loudly carping about the blacklist of the 1950s?

"I've been blackballed from movie roles and television shows because liberal producers don't want me around," Pat Boone is quoted in *New Dimensions* magazine, a conservative publication. "But," he adds, "there are more closet conservatives in the business than anyone realizes. Most of the people who hire and fire are ultra-liberal. You're taking your career in your hands and cutting your own throat if you speak out for the conservative side."

Thus, Hollywood muzzles any effective opposition to its views of the day. In political campaigns, conservatives seldom rally any but major Hollywood names. Despite a great deal of celebrity activism for many causes, George Bush's campaign staff found it impossible to line up much support in Hollywood. Stars like Bob Hope, Tom Selleck, Arnold Schwarzenegger and Chuck Norris are free to endorse a conservative cause, but few minor celebrities have that freedom. Rene Henry, the GOP entertainment coordinator, insists that some conservative celebrities are "misrepresented," while others are just panicked that conservatism could jeopardize, if not ruin, their careers.

"My producers are screaming at me for doing this," Chuck Norris told a *Los Angeles Times* reporter at a Bush fund raiser. At the same time, Cheryl Ladd added, "I think there are a lot of people in this town who are going to vote for George Bush who don't feel comfortable standing up and saying they're going to. Why? Because it's unpopular in the industry!"

On the other hand, liberal democratic candidates have no problem attracting stars and money to their campaigns. Michael Dukakis appealed to many who do most of Hollywood's hiring, firing and deal making: Barry Diller, Chairman of 20th Century-Murdock (aka Fox); Sally Field; Richard Gere; Cher; John Cooke, President of the Disney Channel; Richard Cook, President of Buena Vista Productions; Oliver Stone;

Robert Redford; Tom Hayden; and Frank Wells, President of Disney.

Hundreds of other people lent their names, money and time to Democrat causes through The Hollywood Women's Political Committee, the Show Coalition, Network and other groups.

"There's an unwritten law in Hollywood that makes it very difficult to buck whatever might be 'establishment' and, obviously, it's been known for many years that generally most of the Hollywood establishment are liberal-oriented," concluded Rene Henry.

Tom Selleck, who introduced Nancy Reagan at the Republican Convention in 1988, remarked that those with dissident views in Hollywood are "gun shy. They still have families to support." He told a reporter, "They have to work for a living."

Several months ago, a successful television writer received a letter from the Writers Guild of America-West urging him to join with "People for the American Way" in a lobbying campaign for authorization of taxpayer support for what some have labled "obscene" art. The letter upset the writer since the Writers Guild had obviously decided to utilize membership money to lobby for the National Endowment.

The writer, however, could not speak out publicly against the Guild because of probably repercussions to his career, not so much from his own union, but from the liberals who dominate the industry.

"It would have been professional suicide to speak

out on the other side of that issue," confessed another writer friend of ours. "It's not so much what the Guild would do to you, it's the entire Hollywood community. It's tough enough to get a script read in this town without having political enemies," he added.

In other words, a *de facto* blacklist exists today, even though it is an "informal" list.

Cheryl Rhoden, a spokesperson for the writers' union, in an interview with Joseph Fara of the *Sacramento Union,* dismissed such concerns out of hand. She saw no analogy between the two kinds of blacklisting and told Fara that she believes such fears "are misplaced! People do speak out in Hollywood. Look at Charlton Heston. His views haven't hurt his career." When asked to name another outspoken conservative in Hollywood, however, Rhoden couldn't come up with one.

Another writer described the petition from the Guild as "just another example of the closed mindset of the Hollywood elitists."

Researching this chapter with off-the-record conversations with many acquaintances in the business — and colleagues in the entertainment field — we learned that there are many such examples in Hollywood. Insiders repeatedly told us that anyone who is a political conservative, an outspoken Christian or pro-life is on an "unofficial blacklist." We found few in the oligarchy, some dating back to our school days, who are comfortable talking publicly about this kind of bigotry.

A well known and respected acting coach, an outspoken conservative, says he is constantly vilified by his liberal colleagues. In spite of the insults and occasional blacklisting, he has been able to attract top drawer talent to his classes, working exclusively with referrals.

In Hollywood today, it seems perfectly acceptable for celebrities to make outlandish, irresponsible statements against the United States, the President, conservatives or middle-of-the-roaders. They are even encouraged to do so by their press agents, seeking press on the nightly news.

When producer-writer-director Oliver Stone (*Born on the Fourth of July, Platoon, JFK*) told the *Los Angeles Times* that "America has become a fascist security state and if I were George Bush I'd shoot myself," no one in Hollywood even raised an eyebrow.

If an everyday citizen had made the same statement, the Secret Service would have swarmed all over him, accusing him of encouraging the shooting of a President.

Actor Alec Baldwin topped that statement a few months later. In *Movies* magazine, he told of how he dreamed of finding a "militant organization — like some Black Panther or IRA equivalent — that revolved around some important cause, and going out and blowing up some chemical plant — really put my ass on the line!"

Unlike other industries, there is no price to pay in Hollywood for such bizarre, irrational statements, or support for real left wing activity. There is ample evidence to show that it can actually boost careers and salaries into the million$ of dollar$ per film.

Unlike conservative activism, liberal political activity has great public relations value within the industry and determines whether you work or not. Conservative political activity makes damn sure you are on an unofficial blacklist and do not work at all.

A leading movie magazine, *Premiere,* which is aimed at the industry, commissioned a piece by a well known writer on Cuba's Latin American Film School. She discovered that the school was designed solely to "enhance" Castro's profile in the United States. Its director had lured several Hollywood personalities into aiding the school; Robert Redford, Oliver Stone, George Lucas and Spike Lee were all mentioned in the article.

The school was deemed "free of Castro domination," or so most people in Hollywood had been led to believe. The writer discovered otherwise and wrote accordingly.

After the assigned story was handed in to editor Susan Lyne, the writer was told it could not be used, since the magazine felt some of her sources "were not legitimate or credible." One of the sources was a defector from the film school, who had worked side by side with its director.

Obviously, the article wasn't the pre-conceived

"puff piece" the editors expected. There were obvious political considerations. Those, together with heavy Hollywood magazine advertising, would explain the article's being rejected.

Concern over employment is a major interest to an actor. Acting is a profession at which damn few can make a living, and in which others make millions. There are close to 77,000 members of the Screen Actors Guild, of whom 76% made less than $2,500 working at their professions in 1989.

In 1990, Charlton Heston was asked why those actors, as a segment of the Hollywood establishment, tend to be so liberal.

"It is just not possible for over three quarters of them [actors] to make a decent living as actors. Therefore, if you do make a living, you always feel a little guilty about it...So that tendency among the actors who do make a handsome living in the profession to identify with a cause is perfectly legitimate."

What Heston did not say was that unless actors identify with the "correct" causes and the "correct" political candidates, they might well find themselves within the ranks of the 76% who earn $2,500 or less per year.

It is a sad commentary on what was once a great industry. It is unfortunate that power had become centered in the hands of those who would dictate "correct" political considerations; that is, if people within the industry wish to continue working within the industry.

Unfortunately, any change would incur an 180% swing to the middle of the road. Such a change seems unlikely. We doubt if attitudes will ever change.

CHAPTER TWELVE

"That's a Wrap!" Or Is It?

"Because it is sometimes so unbelievable, the truth often escapes being known."
— **Heraclitus**

Many, many more bizarre tales about Hollywood remain to be told. Not here. Not now. Perhaps later.

Hollywood's sex and raw power can be linked to many of its most blatant scandals over the years. Many powerful people believe that their position of money and the power to hire, fire and make or break stars, producers and directors will deter any adverse opposition. It generally has and always will. Few, if any, people exist within the industry to challenge such bizarre behavior.

There is probably more nonsense hype written about Hollywood than anything else on earth.

Sometimes things go wrong:

On January 8, 1959, the *Los Angeles Mirror-News* (an attempt by the *Los Angeles Times* at an evening edition) ran a front page banner headline:

LIZ TAYLOR A PATIENT IN THE MENINGER CLINIC

The story revealed that Liz Taylor was under observation at the Topeka, Kansas clinic for the emotionally disturbed.

As the papers hit the streets that afternoon, Liz Taylor was in Los Angeles. She had never been to the Meninger Clinic and had no idea of its function. Her press agents, after a hurried press conference at Chasen's restaurant, announced that Taylor was instituting suit against the Times-Mirror Company for printing untrue and defamatory statements.

The next day's editions ran a six column front-page headline: LIZ HERE, NOT IN CLINIC

The article offered the paper's "sincere regrets" for printing the erroneous story, which had originated with a gossip columnist trying to break into the paper. "The mistake resulted in a misunderstanding during a telephone call direct to the Topeka, Kansas, clinic."

Liz Taylor dropped her law suit because, according to her press agent, "One never sues a newspaper in Hollywood!"

It is also advisable to take the printed work with a grain of salt. Many Hollywood journalists consider trade paper reports as "gospel" and regularly quote *The Hollywood Reporter* and *Daily Variety*. Many times, they have been forced to retract.

Trade papers are the most dangerous forms of

documentation extant. They also have the highest "lift factor" by journalists covering the industry than any other publications. One of the first lessons to be learned by neophytes is that distilling facts from the Hollywood trade papers is not dissimilar to deciphering the Dead Sea Scrolls. Producers, directors and performers pay press agents a great deal to get their names in "the trades" on a regular basis, regardless of the subject matter of the item. Many phony picture deals and titles are announced in this fashion, contract signings with unknown producers, all dutifully picked up and reported in other journals. One enterprising press agent, the late Dave Epstein, used the same press releases for years. The only changes were the dates and names to suit his current list of clients. The basic premise remained the same.

We know of no other industry that is able to so rigidly control the media as does the motion picture industry. It has only been since we have ceased maintaining our accreditation that we have been able to write about it as we have. We are no longer restricted by press agents monitoring every interview and can write what we feel, see and can verify.

We also know of no other industry which has managed to invent a creative bookkeeping system that stifles the imagination.

Two unique instances:

When Ricardo Montalban asked Columbia Pictures for his contracted 5% share of *Fantasy Island* profits, he was told, "Sorry, old chap, there are none!" Even though the television series ran for seven years, was syndicated in 42 countries, and is still running somewhere in the world, Montalban was told that the series lost $11 million, an instance roughly equivalent to a car manufacturer building and selling cars at the loss of $100 each for seven years. A car manufacturer wouldn't be in business very long, but the studios manage some of the most creative bean counting in the world — a great deal of it on the edge of the criminal.

Another instance is Paramount Pictures' and Eddie Murphy's *Coming To America*. Putting aside the lawsuit by columnist Art Buchwald and Alan Bernheim, who have been in litigation for five years claiming a share of the profits for their original idea, worldwide, *Coming To America* grossed $250 million in box office receipts.

Paramount received $125 million in rentals (they said).From this, they deducted a Distribution Fee of $42 million, plus Distribution and Marketing "Costs" of $36 million. Deduct production costs of $57 million (including $1,500 for "lunches at McDonalds" while on location) and $5 million in interest.

Paramount says that the film lost money.

Not for Murphy and John Landis, however, who collected all salaries and percentages due them. Paramount Pictures pocketed the $42 million and probably made money on the Distribution and Marketing Costs by using "in house" advertising agencies.

There are many more instances where actors, producers and directors have been removed from profit participation by the creative accounting teams in Hollywood.

However, if you sue the studios, you don't work. Unless you're a major player, you can't beat the oligarchy.

We won't stop talking about it, however! There are many more bizarre stories, vicious exploitation, sexual harassment, devil worship, blacklisting, unexplained deaths and Oscar ripoffs yet to be told.

Epilogue |

"In the Hollywood of the 1930's, the studios were run by pirates, semi-illiterates, amoral immigrants, men who indulged in corruption, blackmail, sex orgies, nepotism, men who made exorbitant profits, bought beautiful women for bit parts, discarded them for younger favorites and trafficked with the most despicable segments of the underworld . . ."

— Lloyd Shearer